A Way With Words

A Way With Words

A GUIDE FOR WRITERS

THOMAS WHISSEN
Wright State University

OXFORD UNIVERSITY PRESS
Oxford   New York   Toronto   Melbourne
1982

Oxford University Press
Oxford London Glasgow
New York Toronto Melbourne
Nairobi Dar es Salaam Cape Town
Kuala Lumpur Singapore Hong Kong Tokyo
Delhi Bombay Calcutta Madras Karachi

and associate companies in
Beirut Berlin Ibadan Mexico City

Library of Congress Cataloging in Publication Data
Whissen, Thomas R.
A way with words.
Includes index.
1. English language—Rhetoric.
2. English language—Style. I. Title.
PE1408.W579 808'.042 81-18974
ISBN 0-19-503041-9 pbk. AACR2

First published as an Oxford University Press paperback, New York, 1982

Printing (last digit): 9 8 7 6 5 4 3 2 1

Printed in the United States of America

Acknowledgments

Lawrence Casler. From "This Thing Called Love Is Pathological" in *Psychology Today Magazine,* December 1969. Copyright © 1969 by Ziff-Davis Publishing Company. Reprinted by permission of the publisher.

E. E. Cummings. From "in Just-," in *Tulips & Chimneys.* Copyright 1923, 1925 and renewed 1951, 1953 by E. E. Cummings. Copyright © 1973, 1976 by Nancy T. Andrews. Copyright © 1973, 1976 by George James Firmage. Reprinted by permission of Liveright Publishing Corporation and Granada Publishing Limited.

Richard A. Lanham. From *Style: An Anti-Textbook.* Copyright © 1974 by Yale University. Reprinted by permission of Yale University Press.

H. L. Mencken. From *The American Language,* Fourth Edition. Copyright © 1963 by Alfred A. Knopf, Inc. Reprinted by permission of Alfred A. Knopf, Inc. From "The National Culture" in *The Yale Review,* June 1920.

Gail Sheehy. From *Passages: Predictable Crises of Adult Life.* Copyright © 1974, 1976 by Gail Sheehy. Reprinted by permission of the publisher, E. P. Dutton, and International Creative Management.

James Thurber. From *My World—And Welcome to It.* Copyright © 1943 by James Thurber. Copyright © 1970 by Helen W. Thurber and Rosemary T. Sauers. Published by Harcourt Brace Jovanovich and reprinted by permission of Mrs. James Thurber.

Tom Wolfe. From "Sliding Down into the Behavioral Sink" from *The Pump House Gang.* Copyright © 1968 by Tom Wolfe. From *Radical Chic* and *Mau-Mauing the Flak Catchers.* Copyright © 1970 by Tom Wolfe. This material first appeared in *The New Yorker.* Reprinted by permission of Farrar, Straus and Giroux, Inc. and International Creative Management.

To my mother
Bertha Madeline Young Whissen
whose love of words
inspired my own

Contents

A Way With Words

Introduction

Style is the way something is put, and people who put things well are said to have "a way with words." It is the purpose of this book to help you have your way with words by increasing your awareness of the many ways language can work for or against you. After you have gone through the exercises in this book, you should be well on the way to acquiring a style that is a more satisfying expression of your thinking and your personality.

Before you can realize your own style, you must first experiment with a variety of styles both good and bad. By analyzing and imitating good style, you learn techniques common to all good writing, for there are certain obligations to language and audience that all good writers share. Equally important to improving your style is a serious and sustained encounter with the elements of bad style. When you analyze and imitate bad style, you learn firsthand what exactly it is that is bad about it and what you can do to avoid it.

The plan of this book is to take you from word to sentence to paragraph to essay in a way that will stretch your imagination and challenge your talents. Along the way you will be asked to experiment with language in new ways. In addition to routine exercises in word usage, sentence structure, and paragraph development, you will be asked to think about the impressions words themselves make on your senses and about the shifts in interpretation words undergo when they are arranged into sentences. You will listen to the cadence of prose and hear the effect it has on style. At times you will find yourself testing, even teasing the language in order to confront it in all its variety.

Throughout this book you will be called on to play a number of roles, constantly exploring the recesses of your personality to discover facets of it you may not have known. You will be sober, playful, grim, whimsical, sad, mad, witty, dull—whatever it takes to release the range of possibilities available to you in developing a style of your own.

In one chapter you may be asked to be icily objective, in another to be embarrassingly personal. You may write in an elegant, polished manner in one lesson and in a loose, rambling manner in the next. The important thing is that you will be learning to write by writing, and the style you ultimately acquire will be a product of all the styles you have written in. As with clothes, you have to try on all possibilities before you can settle on a wardrobe that is versatile enough for any occasion yet remains a true reflection of you.

Although there is a definite plan to the order in which the material in this book is presented, it is quite possible to pick and choose what you can use as you see fit. Less experienced writers, for example, might concentrate on the first half of the book while more experienced writers might concentrate on the last. And any writer, regardless of experience, can skip around at random or dip in at will without fear of violating some sacred design.

Those who can manage it, however, will profit most from a systematic encounter with each section in the order prescribed. Whichever way you approach the book, this is what you will be doing:

In Part I (Impressions) you will examine how words appeal to the senses in ways that carry meaning beyond mere definition.

In Part II (Interpretations) you will discover how suggestive of multiple meanings words can be, depending on the associations you bring to them (connotation) and the contradictions you can either coax from them (ambiguity) or lure them into (irony).

In Part III (Combinations) you will take a new look at sentences, experimenting not only with varieties of sentence structure and style but also with the neglected art of sentence rhythm. You will also see how sentences team up to form paragraphs and how a sentence called in to interact on a team is not the same sentence it was back there by itself on the bench.

In Part IV (Manipulations) you will learn the techniques of the crafty who corrupt style and hoodwink the unsuspecting. By practicing bad style, you will learn not only how to spot it but how to avoid it. Along the way you will find out that writers who confuse, mislead, sidetrack, gush, and commit all manner of crimes against style can be surprisingly charming fellows with more than a trick or two worth learning.

In Part V (Traditions) you will breeze through the last five centuries of English prose style, pausing here and there to parody particular stylistic traits. As you analyze and imitate the stylists of the past, you should acquire a feeling for the changes English prose style has undergone and the way these changes have contributed to the rich variety of stylistic options available to modern writers.

In the final section, Part VI (Transactions), you will be doing exercises in four fundamental contemporary styles. These four styles are intended to serve as a basic repertoire from which you can fashion the style that best suits you and the task at hand. Armed with these options, attuned to the heritage of prose style, alert to the way style can be abused, and aware of the power and personality of words and sentences at work and play, you should be well on your way to becoming the stylist you set out to be.

If you are interested in writing, you know by now that style is more than window dressing. It is not something spread over the content like frosting on a cake. Style is an integral part of content.

The way you say something is as important as (some would say even more important than) what you have to say. Look at the difference between a novel and a plot summary, a poem and a paraphrase, an essay and an abstract. Look at the difference be-tween

>Wide is the gate and broad is the way that leadeth to
>   destruction, and many there be which go in
>   thereat . . .

and

>An awful lot of people are scurrying through the arches
>and skipping merrily down the road to Hell.

The first is solemn, the second irreverent, yet both say essentially the same thing. Those who are in deadly earnest about the first probably think its message is intended for those who take delight in the second. It's all in how you put it, and how you put it is what style is all about.

And now . . . *away with words!*

I

Impressions

Words are the currency of communication, and unless you know how to handle them well, you will shortchange both yourself and your reader. Knowing what you want to say and to whom you want to say it will not get you far if you don't know how to say it, and knowing how begins with a sensitivity to words. Because we are immersed in words in our daily lives, it is very easy to take them for granted and be satisfied with words that come anywhere close to what we mean. Instead of probing for the right word, we grab whatever word is handy, shrug, and say, "Well, you know what I mean."

Since you are already interested in style, you know the real agony of being at a loss for words or stuck for a word or having a word on the tip of your tongue and not being able to spit it out. Even so, you may not be entirely aware of some of the subtler powers words have, powers beyond accuracy of meaning or appropriateness to the context. In addition to what they mean, words have shapes and sounds and rhythms that affect the way they are received and understood. Several words can mean approximately the same thing and yet leave varying impressions depending upon how they look to the eye and how they strike the ear. Moreover, some synonyms have strong associations connected with them that can appeal forcefully to the sense of touch, taste, and smell.

It is the purpose of this section to begin the study of style by concentrating on the sensory impressions words can make. In the three chapters that follow, you will be thinking about and working with words for their own sake. Their context will serve only as a backdrop; the spotlight will be on the words as if, for a while at least, they had an independent life of their own. In a way, of course, they do, but that energy is ordinarily restricted by the demands of the context where words pool their resources in a common cause. Here, as a means of renewing your respect for the authority of the individual word, you will deal with words as if all other elements of style deferred to them. And the best words to use for this purpose are words that appeal to the senses.

1. An Eye for Words

Writing and reading are highly visual activities. The written word can have as great an impact on the eye as on the mind. In poetry and advertising, for example, the way the words look adds significantly to what they say. Some poets even go so far as to arrange the words on the page into illustrations of the meaning.

When the action is ri$^{si^{ng}}$

It isn't sur^{pri}sing
To see people sm$_{i_li}$ng and glad;

But when it is fa$_{ll_{in_g}}$

It's simply ap^{pall}ing

To see them all fr$^{o^{wn_i}}$ng and sad.

Poets of the early seventeenth century used to delight in writing poems in shapes representing the poem's subject matter. Here is one by George Herbert:

A broken ALTAR, Lord, thy servant rears,
Made of a heart, and cemented with tears:
  Whose parts are as thy hand did frame;
  No workman's tool hath touched the same.
      A   HEART   alone
      Is   such   a   stone,
      As   nothing   but
      Thy power doth cut.
      Wherefore each part
      Of   my   hard   heart
      Meets in this frame,
      To praise thy Name:
  That, if I chance to hold my peace,
  These stones to praise thee may not cease.
Oh let thy blessed SACRIFICE be mine,
And sanctify this ALTAR to be thine.

In modern times, e.e. cummings has come to be the poet most noted for arranging the words of a poem in a way that teases the eye.

in Just—
spring   when the world is mud-
luscious the little
lame balloonman

whistles   far   and wee

and eddieandbill come
running from marbles and
piracies and it's
spring

when the world is puddle-wonderful

the queer
old balloonman whistles
far   and   wee
and bettyandisbel come dancing

from hop-scotch and jump-rope and

it's
spring
and
  the

     goat-footed
balloonMan   whistles
far
and
wee

Advertisers are the gurus of the graphic. They know they must catch your eye before they can capture your attention. To them, words are cosmetics, and they know how to make up a label that will dazzle the dollars out of you.

Sometimes they do it with "quaintness":

Ye Olde Gifte Shoppe

Pumblechook's Publick House

Steake and Steinn

Wycliffe Taverne

Grosvenor Greene

Sometimes they do it with "illiteracy":

Tuff-kote caulk

Kwik-kote paint

Redi-kash loans

Sta-prest pants

Dri-kleen spot remover

E-Z-Gro fertilizer

Nite-flite air fares

Sometimes they do it with "cuteness":

Kit Kat Klub

Olive 'r Twist Cocktails

Kuntry Kitchen

Sip 'n' Sup

Knick-Knack Knook

Sometimes they do it with "class":
Lorrimer's Limited
The Regiment for Men
The Squire Shop
Carriage Trade Fashions
Regency Room Exclusives

Sometimes they do it with a curious "foreign flair":
Häagen-Dazs
Paco's Tacos
La Feminique Coiffures
Otto's Auto-Haus

Sometimes they do it with British spellings:
Centre Cinema
Kerb Service
Radial Tyres
Party Favours
Decorator Colours
Programme Guide
The Chelsea Connexion

List some of the eye-catching signs or labels that you have come across:

1. _____

2. _____

3. _____

4. _____

5. _____

Sometimes, as they say, we can't see for looking. We are so used to looking at the written word that we underestimate what we are really seeing. It is not until language calls attention to itself that we are reminded of its visual impact. Take a French menu, for example. Fancy restaurants in this country invariably print their menus in French (*menu*, by the way, is a French word) even though many of them feel obliged to supply an English translation. When they don't, watch out! You may be surprised at what you get. *Soupe du jour* may look appetizing on the menu, but after all, it's only "soup of the day" and might very well turn out to be the kind you hate--or had yesterday.

A lot of people eat with their eyes--and pay through their noses. That is why restaurateurs with an eye to the till will tempt you with this:

Oeufs durs et crudités de la saison

Soupe à l'oignon ou Jus frais de pamplemousse

Saucisses chaudes de Strasbourg sur petits pains chauds, accompagneés de choucroute à l'Alsacienne

Pommes de terre frites et haricots verts du potager

Glace à la fraise ou à la vanille

Café au lait ou Eaux minérales ou carboniseés

when all you are really getting is this:

Hard-boiled eggs and raw vegetables

Onion soup or grapefruit juice

Hot dogs and sauerkraut

French fries and green beans

Ice cream

Coffee or soda pop

Deliberate misspellings are commonly used by advertisers as a means of getting your attention. Like television commercials, the more irritating they are, the more they stick in your mind. Elsewhere, however, misspellings are looked upon as a sign of illiteracy and carefully avoided. "He one the game write after the brake" looks dumb in spite of the student who calls it "creative." Even shortcuts like "thru" and "nite" only make a writer look lazy or coy. Good writers conform to the accepted spelling rules of their times. However, rules do change, and sometimes we find that a manuscript from the past gains added charm solely by virtue of its archaic spelling.

Since there were no spelling rules to speak of in Chaucer's day, we cannot accuse him of misspelling; he had to trust to his ear, his eye, and his imagination to write in the dialect that was to become the official court language we now call Middle English. Today, Chaucer's English looks very strange to us, and at first glance the untrained eye may find it incomprehensible. When we look more closely, we realize that it is largely the odd spelling that distracts us. Within that spelling is a language not very far removed from our own, and with a little practice we can learn to read Chaucer with a fair degree of ease. There are those, in fact, who ultimately find Chaucer's spelling one of the most appealing things about him. The eighteenth-century literati called him a barbarian, but since the age of the Romantics, readers have been enchanted by the very qualities the wits deplored, not the least of which is the way the words look on the page.

Here are a few charming lines from the Prologue to the *Canterbury Tales:*

> So hote he loved that by nightertale
> He slepte namore than dooth a nightingale.
>
> Housbondes at chirche dore she hadde five,
> Withouten other compaignye in youthe—

Thomas Chatterton was an eighteenth-century poet who poisoned himself at the age of seventeen after perpetrating a rather remarkable hoax on the literary world. To satisfy a growing underground taste for medieval poetry, Chatterton pretended to have discovered some poems by one Thomas Rowley, a nonexistent monk, poet, and antiquarian of the fifteenth century. Chatterton was exposed and persecuted by the literary establishment, but the later Romantics revered him as a neglected genius, calling him that "marvellous boy," and venerating him as a martyr to poetry. Here is a stanza from Chatterton's "Mynstrelles Songe." What do you think?

> Harke! the ravenne flappes hys wynge,
> In the briered delle belowe;
> Harke! the dethe-owle loude dothe synge,
> To the nyghte-mares as heie goe;
>   Mie love ys dedde,
>   Gon to hys dethe-bedde,
>   Al under the wyllowe tree.

Turn this doggerel into an "aulde ballade" by antiquating the spelling:

> His heart upon his sleeve does bleed
> His lady fair has fled;
> He mops his brow and sips his mead
> And then he goes to bed.

_____

_____

_____

_____

Poets may still experiment with spelling, but prose writers seldom tamper with it. A few, among whom James Joyce is the most prominent, have compressed or distended or sandwiched words in ways that cause the words to call attention to themselves, but such inventiveness is only marginally a matter of spelling, and most efforts in this direction have met with limited success. There are ordinary words, however, that do seem to look like what they mean and which, when used in the right spot, can "illustrate" their meaning.

Take a *look* at these sentences:

1. He was a squat little man.

   "Little" does not *look* little, but "squat" *looks* squat. The "l's" and "t's" in "little" make it look tall and thin, but the first four letters of "squat" are short and fat.

2. He was a tall thin man.

   "Tall" and "thin" *look* tall and thin. And "fat" looks *fat.*

3. The clouds scudded across the sky.

   Certainly "scudded" *sounds* like clouds sort of bumping and jostling their way across the sky, but the three "d's," close together as they are, *look* like the piling up and pushing ahead of rapidly moving clouds.

4. The prisoners huddled in the corner.

   The "ddl" are letters that, themselves, seem to huddle in the middle of the word.

We like expressions like "fiddle-faddle," "hodge-podge," "helter-skelter," and "hanky-panky" as much for their *looks* as for their *sound.* What similar expressions would you insert in the following sentences:

1. Never having any fun makes for a _____
   monotonous
   existence.

2. Hurry up! Don't_____!
   dawdle

3. Let's dig through the window dressing and get right down to
   the_____.
   dirt

4. Chubby? Pudgy? Why she's downright_____
   short and fat

5. Nobody likes to ask him to help make a decision because he's
   so_____.
   vacillating

Although it's easy sometimes to *think* that a word looks like the thing it stands for merely because of a familiar association between the two, there are words that actually *do* resemble the object they represent. When it is possible to use such a word, the impact on the reader is reinforced by the word's appearance.

Here are a few examples.

1. He stuck a toothpick into a *tidbit*.
2. He was about to *pop* the *tidbit* into his mouth when he saw he was being observed.
3. She made a few *squiggles* on the page and then gave up.
4. To her a necklace was little more than a *gewgaw*.
5. It was hard to keep it *even*; it kept *tilting* to the right.

What visually representative words can you think of to dress up the following sentences?

1. He tried to hold the tray perfectly_____.

straight
2. He concluded that the lines were not exactly_____
   _____.
equidistant
3. She_____a hole in the sleeve.

cut
4. Suddenly he felt_____in his knees.

unsteady
5. He thought she said it just to_____him.

tickle
6. In her dreams the irrepressible_____was always limping after her.

small demon
7. When he remarked on the tintinnabulation following the assassination, she accused him of wanting to_____her stutter.

mock

If you want to emphasize a word, and you feel that the word alone does not call sufficient attention to itself, there are a number of devices you may use to increase the word's visibility. Some of these devices depend on the typesetter's art, but even they can be simulated by hand or at the typewriter. Among them are such things as the use of quotation marks, italics, and foreign words.

Quotation Marks

The primary purpose of quotation marks is, of course, to indicate a quotation. Beyond this, however, they are good for calling attention to a word that is being used in a special sense, usually an ironic one, that the writer trusts the reader to "get." ("Get" is in quotation marks here because although it is a synonym for "understand," it also suggests the special ability of being able to "catch on" quickly to nuances others less astute might overlook.) Notice the use of quotation marks in the following examples:

1. Everyone wondered what she meant when she told them her son was on a "trip."
2. The mother looked disconcerted when the principal told her that her son was an "exceptional" child.
3. Mark Antony insisted repeatedly that Brutus and his fellow conspirators were all "honorable" men.
4. The student felt flattered when the teacher told him that his writing was "unique."
5. It didn't take him long to learn what they meant when they told him that a spoiled wife would be a "dear" companion.

As you can see, the words in quotation marks are usually ambiguous. What the quotation marks do is to stress the less apparent, or secondary, meaning of the word. In the following sentences, put quotation marks around the ambiguous words that you think need their less apparent, or secondary, meaning stressed.

1. Wives have traditionally been the best bargain a man could get.
2. The whole set-up struck him as rather funny.
3. He had a taste for adult movies.
4. Dante had a comic vision of man's destiny.
5. She said she preferred men who were mature.

Quotation marks are also used to indicate the use of understatement, especially when such understatement might otherwise be lost on the reader. Note the following:

1. The patient, so they were told, died of "complications."
2. The Englishman spoke unhappily of the recent "unpleasantness" in the Middle East.

3. Although it was a blatant breach of security, the intelligence officer was accused only of having "misplaced" the documents.
4. Richard Nixon was forced to resign because of "unfortunate circumstances."
5. After the discovery of the twelve bodies in the shallow grave, the inspector declared that he suspected "foul play."

Italics

Italics are used as a means of stressing key words either to emphasize a specific meaning or to exaggerate an accepted one. For example:

1. A table is a thing, a word, and a sound. Is there a connection between the *word* table, the *thing* table, and the *sound* table?
2. Most of what we call *knowledge* is, in fact, only *information*.
3. True *ignorance* is not stupidity; it is lack of awareness. To remain deliberately ignorant is sheer *stupidity*.
4. Malcontents are forever claiming *intimidation*.
5. Educators used to boast that they didn't teach subject matter, they taught *children*.

Which word or words would you italicize in each of the following sentences?

1. Universal brotherhood has always been a highly romantic dream.
2. What one side called civil disobedience, the other called criminal disobedience.
3. The guru claimed not to have gone merely to the edge of reality but actually beyond.
4. She isn't merely intrigued by witchcraft; she's possessed by it.
5. The court was appalled when the killer described his deed not as an act of revenge but as an act of justice.

Italics are also used to indicate voice stress in sentences that might otherwise be misread.

1. It's not that I don't know *how* perverts do it; it's that I don't know how they *do* it.
2. What's the matter with *him?*
3. Do you *have* to be at the station by nine?
4. I wouldn't even want to go *up* to the attic, let alone go *in* it.
5. Where do you want me to hang *this* picture?

Underline the word you would stress in each of the following sentences in order to alter the meaning.

1. Do you ever think about me?
2. I don't know where I'm going to put your things.
3. She said she loved me.
4. He asked me to do it.
5. Why do you always do this to me?

Foreign Words

The inclusion of a foreign word or phrase, particularly when it appears in italics, always calls attention to itself—too much sometimes. For that reason, foreign expressions ought to be used sparingly and wisely, even when they are ones that have become common to the English language. Often, as in many of the following examples, they are used for ironic effect.

1. He explained that French cooking was not his *forte.*
2. Her employer gave her *carte blanche* in the redecorating of the office.
3. The couple was discovered *in flagrante delicto.*
4. To him she was nothing but a *Hausfrau.*
5. On occasion she liked to go slumming among *hoi polloi.*
6. She said she could not live without him, that he was her *sine qua non.*
7. Painting was his hobby, he said, not his *métier.*

8. She found her kidnapper to be very *simpatico*.
9. We could continue this exercise *ad infinitum*.
10. We have already continued it *ad nauseam*.

Complete the following sentences by the use of appropriate foreign words or expressions. You may have to consult a dictionary.

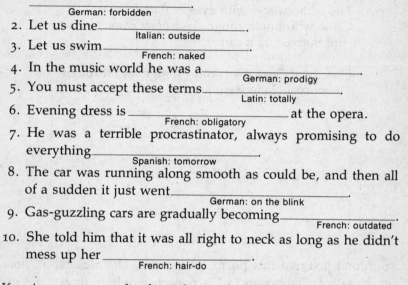

1. She told him that his presence in her house was strictly_____
   _____.
   German: forbidden

2. Let us dine_____.
   Italian: outside

3. Let us swim_____.
   French: naked

4. In the music world he was a_____.
   German: prodigy

5. You must accept these terms_____.
   Latin: totally

6. Evening dress is _____ at the opera.
   French: obligatory

7. He was a terrible procrastinator, always promising to do everything_____.
   Spanish: tomorrow

8. The car was running along smooth as could be, and then all of a sudden it just went_____.
   German: on the blink

9. Gas-guzzling cars are gradually becoming_____.
   French: outdated

10. She told him that it was all right to neck as long as he didn't mess up her _____.
    French: hair-do

Keeping an eye out for the right word is the hallmark of the good stylist. Words are his colors, his clay, and when he chooses them, he will not overlook the visual impression they can make on the reader.

2. An Ear for Words

'Twas brillig, and the slithey toves
Did gyre and gimble in the wabe;

The Jabberwock, with eyes of flame,
Came whiffling through the tulgey wood,
And burbled as it came!

One, two! One, two! And through and through
The vorpal blade went snicker-snack!

LEWIS CARROLL
"Jabberwocky"

You don't just *read* this poem, you *hear* it. Often called a "nonsense" poem, "Jabberwocky" is nonsense only to those who exclude the "senses" from their definition of sense. For its appeal to the senses—particularly the sense of hearing—is unmistakable. Its meaning is clear enough to the ear. What makes it so marvelously provocative is the fact that its language is not pinned down to dictionary definitions. Its meaning goes beyond definition to elicit responses from somewhere deep down in our subconscious, the only place where some say meaning exists at all. To them, dictionary definitions are mere pale attempts to verbalize the preconscious origins of meaning. What we respond to in language, they contend, is less to some abstract "meaning" and more to its concrete *sound*.

For example, "vacillate" *sounds* wishy-washy; "indecisive" does not. "Flaccid" (pronounced *flak-sid*) doesn't sound limp; mis-pronounced *flas-sid,* it does. You won't find it difficult to under-stand how a twelve-year-old boy once wrote this beginning to a ghost story: "The wind howled scrupulously through the trees." Just *listen* to "scrupulously" and you will hear what he heard: something chilling and ominous.

Onomatopoeia is the term we use to identify words that imitate sounds. A few common ones are *ping-pong, ding-dong, babble, croak, sizzle, murmur, mumble.* These words are the result of de-liberate attempts to imitate familiar sounds. You can hear the sound the word is identifying in *buzz, hiss,* and *whirr.* In addi-tion to these direct imitations there are words that have other origins but still tend to suggest the sound of the things they are identifying. You can "hear" the meaning in such words as *crack, whip, crunch,* and *squish.* And don't forget *snap, crackle,* and *pop.*

Since we hear long before we ever learn to read, our responses to the way words sound are spontaneous and immediate. Sound triggers other sensory responses (taste, touch, smell) and finally influences the way we read. When we first see words, we delight in their shapes; but once we begin to read, we learn the words by associating the sounds. Sometimes reading even dulls the sensory experience of language. As we read, we forget to listen— or even to look. We forget that childish delight we took in the sheer sound of words, back when we didn't demand rational meaning because we could "feel" what the words meant. How-ever, this feeling for words remains with us the rest of our lives, try as we might to subdue it in favor of intellectual responses. The truth of this is borne out by the fact that when we complain that something we are reading is dry and dull, what is really wrong is that what we are reading simply lacks any appeal to the senses—and particularly to the sense of hearing. It is abstract and cerebral, not concrete and visceral.

The English Romantic poets knew this well, and that is why they wrote lines like:

> Her rich attire creeps rustling to her knees.   (Keats)

Rather than:

> A little learning is a dangerous thing.   (Pope)

Good prose writers, too, know the value of the sound of words and are unafraid to use language that appeals strongly to the ear. Words like "splatter" and "thwack" and "grumble" and "slouch" can make the reader sit up and take notice.

Here are some examples of the use of sound simulation.

1. The tires *squealed* as the car rounded the corner.
2. Two girls were *giggling* in the back of the room.
3. They nestled cozily before a *crackling* fire.
4. The horse's hooves *clattered* on the cobblestones.
5. The twig *snapped* beneath his foot.

Find synonyms for the words in parentheses that simulate the sound of the word's referent.

1. Drop by drop the water_____on the page.

(fell)
2. He was driven almost mad by the_____of the unoiled wheel.

(grating sound)
3. The_____of the tires told him that the car had turned the corner fast.

(shrill sound)
4. He bent down so that she could_____something in his hear.

(softly say)
5. The old man began to_____and cough.

(breathe noisily)

Test these examples of *sound simulation* on your ear:

1. He shuddered as he *squashed* the bug beneath his foot.
2. The tired student *slumped* in his chair.
3. She *cringed* whenever that creep came near her.
4. He was the creep who *popped* her balloon.
5. A lack of money put a *crimp* in his plans.

Try your "ear" at these sentences:

1. The hawk _____ down on its prey.
2. The egg burst and _____ all over the kitchen.
3. The drool came _____ out of the baby's mouth.
4. The snake _____ along the ground.
5. He was so handsome, she thought she was going to _____ at his feet.

The appeal to the sense of hearing goes, of course, beyond sound simulation. It includes any device a writer can find to make the reader *listen* to what he is reading. The most common devices are: rhyme, alliteration, assonance, consonance, and dissonance.

Rhyme

People usually associate rhyme with poetry and let it go at that. Little do they realize how much internal rhyme is present in a flowing and melodious line of good prose. Writers rarely rhyme words consciously within a line, however. What happens, it seems, is that a word in one part of the sentence inspires its echo in another part of the sentence, and the writer finds himself using a rhyming word without any deliberate intention whatsoever. At least that's the way it seems. Call it talent, call it accident, the point is that it happens. And if it isn't happening to you, why shouldn't you be a little self-conscious about it for a while and maybe improve your style? You don't want to overdo it, certainly, but there's no doubt that the discreet use of internal rhyme in a line of prose can make it more agreeable to the ear, more rhythmic, more balanced.

Notice the effect of rhyming words in the following examples.

1. Just because he is ill does not mean that we will rush to fill his post.
2. This may be his worst move ever, but it doesn't mean we're ready yet to sever the relationship.

3. It's those up front who get the brunt of the criticism.
4. It soon became quite clear that they had nothing really to fear from his presence among them.
5. He was wrong once, and it won't be long before he'll be wrong again.
6. He's fat because he sat in that chair too long.
7. He was a poor father because it was always too much bother to play with his kids.
8. What you've got to prove is the validity of the undertaking.
9. It doesn't make sense to talk now of immense projects.
10. I have a high regard for any man who's willing to try.
11. The price is what is so very nice about it.
12. He tried to explain that it was not his style to entertain unimportant people.
13. He planned to expand the business rapidly.
14. His plea was that they let things be until the coast was clear.
15. His understanding was that the opposition was demanding too much.
16. He was quite right about the site of the new building.
17. She claimed it wasn't fair to have to share her earnings with him.

Insert a word in each sentence that rhymes with some other word in the same sentence.

1. As an agent, he went wherever he was _____.
2. He was told that he was too _____ for the job.
3. The side of the mountain was too steep for him to be able to _____ his balance.
4. She said she wouldn't mind if he could just _____ someone to take care of the house.
5. There were so few she could turn to who could actually _____ anything about it.
6. You have to _____ an entire block before you come to it.

7. It seems that we ought to be able to _____ on something for the bride.

8. It might be better if we just go ahead and _____ have her way.

9. This might be the best work you've _____, but don't think it means you've won the award.

10. I thought it was very _____ of him to meet us at the station.

Alliteration

Alliteration is the repetition of initial sounds in two or more words: Simple Simon, Peter Pan, Jack and Jill. Here are some alliterative sentences you may be familiar with:

1. Seven slippery slimy snakes slipping slowly sideways.
2. The big black bug bled bitter black blood on the big barn door.
3. Amiable Amy ambled airily around the apple arbor.

Try making up one of your own by completing the following sentences.

1. Red rubber rings _____
2. Two tacky tables _____
3. If Ivan isn't _____

Alliteration is, of course, the essence of the humor in word play like this. These sentences are tongue-twisters (notice the alliteration) and quickly demonstrate that a little alliteration goes a long way. Even those who deplore alliteration know that there is something seductive about it that can lure even the most stalwart into an occasional abuse. Writers are particularly vulnerable when they are listing items in a series. If the first two words in the series just happen to begin with the same letter, the temptation to continue the alliteration is almost irresistible.
How are you inclined to finish these sentences?

1. Iago was callous, conniving, and _____ .
2. He was an aggressive man: big, bold, and _____ .
3. The film was disgusting, distasteful, and _____ .

Alliteration is a common poetic device which, when used wisely, can heighten the effect without being embarrassing. For example:

> He clasps the crag with crooked hands.
>   (Tennyson's "Eagle")

> Because the Holy Ghost over the bent
> World broods with warm breast and with ah!
>   bright wings.
>   (Hopkins' "God's Grandeur")

> If to her share some female errors fall,
> Look on her face, and you'll forget 'em all.
>   (Pope's "The Rape of the Lock")

Old English poets depended exclusively upon alliteration for rhyme. They called it head-rhyme, and they had it all carefully worked out so that the stressed words in each line began with the same sound. It resulted in a lot of stretching of the imagination—and a lot of monotony. Here's an example rendered in modern English.

> Bring me my bowl of burning gold
> And gladly guide my greedy hand
> Which Heaven hastens to a holy fire
> Fed by flames that fury fans.

Good poets since then have toned down such blatant alliteration, although Shakespeare was goaded in his day to make fun of alliterative excesses:

> Whereat, with blade, with bloody blameful blade.
> He bravely broach'd his boiling bloody breast.
>   (from *A Midsummer Night's Dream*)

Nevertheless, when used well, alliteration can produce the musical, hypnotic effect Tennyson was after in these lines from "Come Down, O Maid":

> the children call, and I
> Thy shepherd pipe, and sweet is every sound,
> Sweeter thy voice, but every sound is sweet;
> Myriads of rivulets hurrying through the lawn,
> The moan of doves in immemorial elms,
> And murmuring of innumerable bees.

Some novelists like alliterative titles while others go out of their way to avoid them. Such titles were quite popular in the early days of the novel: *Roderick Random, Peregrine Pickle, Rob Roy, Pride and Prejudice, Sense and Sensibility.* Nowadays we find such titles restricted to books like *Harvest Home, The Peter Principle,* and *Components of Composition.*

While prose writers will also avoid such alliterative clichés as "dead as a doornail," "hale and hearty," "cool as a cucumber," "lewd and lascivious," they are not above an occasional adjective that begins with the same sound as the word it describes: lovely lady, mean man, wicked weather, tender touch, cool kiss, sick sensation, clammy cold, great guy, terrific team, proud parents, wayward wives.

An alliterative adjective, however, is most effective when the adjective is a word or two away from the noun it describes. For example:

1. The teacher grew tired of the lesson.
2. The passengers found the delays extremely depressing.
3. The celebration was enormously successful.
4. The prisoner was too proud to knuckle under.
5. That woman is absolutely wonderful with children.

For the indicated words supply synonyms that begin with the same sound as the nouns they describe.

1. She wanted a companion who was _____.
   agreeable

2. The design on the china is extremely _____.
   frail

3. His mind was so_____that he couldn't think
   confused
   clearly.

4. The sound of the guns was_____to his ears.
   nauseating

5. She complained that her neighbors were too_____.
   loud

Alliteration is not restricted, of course, to adjectives and nouns in tandem. Two nouns may be alliterative (bed and board, house and home, women and wine, rock and roll) or two adjectives (sane and sound, bright and breezy, calm and collected, short and sweet) or two adverbs (quickly and quietly, boldly and bravely, slowly but surely) or two verbs (do or die, sink or swim, rant and rave, aid and abet) as well as all imaginable combinations therewith. Nor are alliterative combinations limited to two words, but more than two defeat the purpose of alliteration in prose, which is to form a casual link (a transition) between parts of a sentence and thus tighten the construction of the sentence.

Find a synonym for the indicated words that begin with the same sound as the word that is italicized:

1. Some thought her *nasty;* others thought her_____.
2. Will it be *clear,* or will it be _____?   pleasant
   overcast

3. He said he would be_____just to get a *glimpse* of
   happy
   her studio.

4. He *thought* it over carefully before he_____it out.
   tossed

5. *Stealthily* the hunter_____his prey.
   pursued

Assonance

Assonance is the use of identical vowel sounds preceded and followed by different consonant sounds. For example: hide-mine, throat-soak, blot-clod, drain-blade, farm-hard, curl-heard, broil-moist, loud-clout, grand-black, crude-tune, mud-run, grist-ship, throttle-bottom, sick-prince. Here are some familiar assonant expressions: hat rack, shop talk, jail bait, bake sale, lug nut, home phone.

See if you can think up a few examples of assonance.

1. _____

2. _____

3. _____

4. _____

5. _____

Look closely at the use of assonance in these examples:

1. The runner stumbled over his own foot.
2. The hatchet was planted between his eyes.
3. The joggers were robbers in disguise.
4. He put his crew socks in the shoe box.
5. The coin made a ringing noise as it dropped.

Supply assonant synonyms to complete the following sentences.

1. He vowed he was_____sober at the time.
   utterly
2. He wanted to make a_____trip to the store.
   fast
3. She was behaving like a_____lady.
   deranged
4. They heard a_____growl at the door.
   noisy
5. The bride had a big _____on her face.
   grin

As you might expect, poets are particularly fond of assonance. Not only does it make the transition smoother between words, it also enhances the mood of a sentence. Notice how the mood is established and sustained in each line of the following quatrain by means of the repetition of the vowel sounds.

Straying by the graveyard on a rainy April day,
He loathed the old and mouldy stones and so was loath
    to stay;
But once the sun came out and brushed his upturned
    face with May
He deemed it mean and sneaky just to up and steal
    away.

Circle the related assonant combinations in the following paragraph.

The man looked sadly at the depressing spectacle of his nor-
mally quiet wife making a crazy fool of herself. There she was,
unashamedly straddling the piano bench, hands fanning the air,
feet keeping time with the rhythm of the distraught pianist, who
was gallantly pounding out the crude tune she had demanded
while bravely trying to maintain his place beside her. This was
hardly the party he had looked forward to, and now he bowed
his head and waited patiently for the inevitable end when she
would clap her hands, stand up to dance, and collapse like a
punctured lung.

Consonance

Consonance is the use of parallel consonant sounds to enclose
differing vowel sounds in two or more nearby words. For example: fail-feel, rough-roof, ruin-rain, jog-jig, groan-grin, wait-wit,
seed-sad, mill-mole, trouble-treble, loud-load, simple-sample,
listen-loosen, bench-bunch, limp-lump. Some common expressions are good examples of consonance: fiddle-faddle, pitter-
patter, dilly-dally, wishy-washy, mish-mash, flim-flam, ship-
shape, knick-knack, tip-top, rag-rug.

Consonance can sometimes be more of an embarrassment than
a help. Certain combinations just simply have to be avoided because they ruin any attempt at a serious effect. Take these, for

example: bitter butter, solid salad, sour sewer, green grain, black block, sweet sweat, pitch patch, larger ledger, holy holly, spare spur, group gripe.

Because they tend to sound silly or jingly in tandem, consonant words, like alliterative words, are more effective when they are separated from each other. The trick is to keep the consonant words just far enough apart to achieve the desired effect. See how successfully you think consonance is employed in the following examples.

1. When dresses were first shortened, knees were news.
2. In Robin Hood's day a friar was considerably freer to do whatever pleased him.
3. It was a fight resolved by fate.
4. He lost his bet on the last bout.
5. Pick up a pack at your local carry-out.
6. After he lost, he vowed that he would avoid the tables forever.
7. You have nothing to gain by carrying a gun.
8. If you lose, there are laws to protect you.
9. Too much cheer and the chair will elude you.
10. The boys went straight for the booze.
11. If you win, there will be wine.
12. The gnome was numb with cold.
13. This drill is becoming a bit droll.
14. A French cook never trifles with the truffles.
15. She said she hated to dance with a dunce.
16. You can sleep in your slip; but don't nod in the nude.
17. This above all: don't let anyone steal your style.

Fill in the blanks in the following sentences with words that are in consonance with the words that are italicized:

1. The marching band _____ across the *field*.
2. The *band* found itself in a financial _____ .
3. Excessive *grease* makes food look _____ .

4. One of his *games* was massaging his _____.
5. He tried unsuccessfully to *pawn* his _____.
6. Of what we call *glamour* she had nary a _____.
7. His attempt to use *force* was a _____.
8. When asked if they approved his *grant*, all he got was a _____.
9. To be truly *devout*, you must _____ much time to prayer.
10. He thought he could *settle* the matter by being extremely _____ _____.
11. When they *manned* the lifeboats, his _____ went blank.
12. She thought her nerves would *shatter* at the rattling of the _____.
13. It's a despicable person who would *burn* a farmer's _____.
14. When you mill and plane *lumber*, your muscles become _____ _____.
15. The cook began to *growl* when he took a look at his dirty _____.
16. At graduation the valedictorian did nothing but *tussle* with his _____.
17. The cook _____ about how many times he *basted* the turkey.

Dissonance

Dissonance is the use of harsh or inharmonious combinations of sounds. Obviously, such sounds are ordinarily to be avoided. Usually, when dissonance does occur, it is unintentional and a sure sign of bad style. However, there are certain times when dissonance can engage the reader's attention in such a way as to communicate something the writer can find no better way to express. When you come across the effective use of dissonance, you know immediately that it is done deliberately, not accidentally.

In the following examples, dissonance is somewhat overdone for the purpose of compressing and illustrating its effect. Can you explain how it works?

1. Shards of shrapnel struck like lightning.
2. When the water froze, the crock cracked and fell apart.
3. His parched throat ached.
4. Mud chunks clung to his boots.
5. Squat shrubs blocked the track.
6. The taut rope snapped in his hands.
7. The gears stripped as the clutch jammed.
8. The gun butt jerked as he fired.
9. Three shrill blasts split the silence.
10. Sharp rocks scraped his skin.

Dissonance is a staccato assault on the eardrums. When you come across it while reading, you are forced to slow down and feel the impact of the words as they approximate the actual experience they are describing. Poets want you to slow down when you read poetry, anyway, so they take every opportunity they can to put words together that make fast reading difficult. Read the following lines from Matthew Arnold aloud and listen to the effect of the dissonance:

> A bolt is shot back somewhere in our breast
> And a lost pulse of feeling stirs again.
> The eye sinks inward, and the heart lies plain,
> And what we mean, we say, and what we would, we
>   know.

It would hardly be fair to call that last line dissonant, in the sense of "jarring," but because it forces you to give equal stress to each syllable, you must depart from the ordinary rhythms of speech to get from the line what it says. Notice the solemn progression of monosyllables along with the use of assonance and alliteration. All these devices combine to give the line an unmistakable ten-

sion. Here is a dissonant line from Arnold that is not so successful:

> Who prop, thou ask'st, in these bad days, my mind?

There is just no decent way to read this line and not make both
it and the question is poses ludicrous. Even Coleridge in the immortal "Kubla Khan" is not free of the curse of unintentional
dissonance:

> And from this chasm, with ceaseless turmoil seething,
> As if this earth in fast thick pants were breathing—

Of course, the imagery doesn't help much either.
  Gerard Manley Hopkins is the poet who made dissonance his
trademark by perfecting it as a highly provocative poetic technique. Just feel the power that accrues to these lines as the dis-
cordant sounds accumulate in mounting cacophony:

> Glory be to God for dappled things—
>   For skies of couple-colour as a brinded cow;
>   For rose-moles all in stipple upon trout that swim;
> Fresh-firecoal chestnut-falls; finches' wings;
>   Landscape plotted and pieced—fold, fallow, and
>   plough;
>   And all trades, their gear and tackle and trim.
> All things counter, original, spare, strange;
>   Whatever is fickle, freckled (who knows how?)
>   With swift, slow; sweet, sour; adazzle, dim;
> He fathers-forth whose beauty is past change:
>   Praise him.

Do your best to find some dissonant words that contribute to the
staccato effect that these sentences call for.

1. When he slammed on the brakes, her neck _____
   violently.

2. At the sound of the alarm, the marching troops _____ and fled for cover.
3. He crawled painfully across the _____ stretch of desert.
4. She gasped as she heard the _____ crunch of shattered glass.
5. He shivered in the _____ gloom of the cell.

Words are sound effects. Language begins in sound, and a good stylist will remember that when he converts sounds to symbols. A reader "hears" what he sees, and well-chosen language can affect his ear as certainly as if he were being read aloud to. In fact, a good test of style is to read your prose aloud. Often when we are writing, we will go back over what we have written, frown, and say, "It just doesn't *sound* right." Then we rewrite until it does.

Words are a writer's musical notes; their sound is often their sense.

3. A Feel, a Taste, and a Nose for Words

Whereas words do have shapes that we can see and sounds that we can hear, when they stimulate the other senses—touch, taste, smell—they do so only because of associations we have learned to make between them. As children, we smelled decayed meat, were told it was "rancid," and thereafter associated the word "rancid" with the smell of decay until the word itself seemed to convey that impression. Repeated experience with smooth surfaces made the word "smooth" come to feel smooth. This is not to say that the word itself does not have a certain quality of smoothness to it. The quiet "m," the long "oo," the soft "th" actually sound, and therefore "feel," smooth, especially if we drag the word out. In this case, the look and the sound of the word contribute to the sensation of feeling already there by association.

"Pierce" and "perforate" are synonyms, but because "pierce" sounds more painful than "perforate," it seems to "feel" more painful. The single syllable is shrill and abrupt, a scream of pain as the needle jabs into the skin; "jabs," by the way, not "penetrates," because "jab" is sharper and hurts more. "Clammy" sounds, and therefore feels, chillier and damper than "moist";

"fetid" smells worse than "smelly"; "mellow" tastes smoother than "full flavored."

All of us who share a language have an immense vocabulary of highly descriptive words that give us the impression that we are actually experiencing the sensation of the thing described through the description itself. These words are among the most basic in the language, and the wise stylist is the one who will not neglect their power to affect the reader.

As you go through the following exercises in the use of these richly suggestive words, think carefully about your choices and be prepared to explain them. Why "sticky" and not "gooey"? Why "aroma" and not "scent"? Why "tart" and not "bitter"?

The Sense of Touch

Here are some words that seem to "feel" like what they represent:

1. *Undulate* insinuates itself in and around, over and under. It curves and coils.
2. *Slither* glides with slime and stealth.
3. *Slimy* is slippery and clammy.
4. *Slobber* slurps and blobs, drools and blubbers.
5. *Textured* is balanced, patterned, embossed, rich, luxuriant.

Exercise
Supply words that "feel" like what they represent.

1. His ingratiating manner was the product of a beguiling smile and a _____ tongue.
2. The newly waxed floor was _____ under her feet.
3. The creamy ale was _____ to his nerves.
4. He winced as the pliers _____ his finger.
5. His scalp _____ as the noise came closer.

The language is overflowing with verbs that convey tactile impressions. Observe the following:

Example
1. His arm *throbbed* with the pain of the needle.
2. The rabbit's throat *pulsated* with fear.
3. The dampness *clawed* at his throat.
4. The failure *pricked* his inflated ego.
5. He screamed when the nerve was *pinched*.
6. The very thought of it *tickled* his funny bone.
7. The irate detective *choked* the confession out of the killer.
8. Our egos need to be *stroked* occasionally.
9. She was *torn* between marriage and a career.
10. The poor woman was *lacerated* by the pitiless scorn of her accuser.

Exercise
Supply a verb that helps these sentences make a stronger or more suggestive tactile impression.

1. His wife _____ him on to higher and higher achievement.

pushed
2. The police _____ a murder rap on him.

laid
3. It seemed to him that he had been _____ on long enough by his opponents.

stepped
4. The wail of the siren _____ his eardrums.

penetrated
5. Fear _____ at the foundation of his courage.

ate away
6. He was _____ by emotion when he saw her display of courage.

held
7. He felt his whole body _____ with fear.

tighten
8. His heart was _____ with anguish.

assaulted
9. Slowly the oil _____ out through the cracks.

leaked
10. When the earthquake struck, he could feel the whole building _____ beneath him.

move

There are also many good nouns you can use to add "feeling" to your writing.

Example
1. Fame is the *spur*.

2. A *spasm* of envy shook him when he saw what the other man had.
3. A *twinge* of nostalgia almost made him lose control.
4. He knew the *ache* of a lost love.
5. It was sheer *torture* to imagine what she was up to.

Exercise
Supply nouns to the following sentences to increase their tactile appeal.

1. The boxer was stunned by the unexpected _____ to his jaw.

blow
2. Aren't you itching to scratch that irresistible _____?

craving
3. It was with a _____ that she touched the corpse.

vibrating motion
4. He felt a severe _____ in the pit of his stomach.

hunger pain
5. She wept from the _____ of his bitter rebuke.

smart

And, of course, there are always good adjectives and adverbs around to intensify the tactile effect of a sentence.

Example
1. His voice was as *scratchy* as steel wool.
2. They had *plush* carpet throughout the house.
3. Suddenly she went *limp* in his arms.
4. He rubbed the *gritty* soap between his hands.
5. His hands slid along her *oily* skin.

Exercise
Choose some adjectives and adverbs of your own to give these sentences a more immediate sense of touch.

1. The _____ texture of the glossy magazine cover was cool against her arms.

slippery smooth
2. The victim was killed by a blow on the head from a _____ _____ instrument.

heavy, thick, dull

3. His scalp crawled with a _____ sensation.
                                        stinging
4. Her attitude was as _____ as glass.
                                hard, firm
5. She felt those _____ fingers up and down her spine.
                        cold

Frequently we use figurative language (metaphors and similes) to describe tactile impressions. Notice how the borrowing of such words from other contexts helps to sharpen the tactile impression by means of comparison.

Example
1. When he saw the gun, his legs turned to *jelly* (or *rubber*).
2. The cosmetics gave her a *creamy* complexion.
3. Her skin was *satin* to his touch.
4. He was caught in a *web* of circumstances.
5. Shaking hands with him was like *reaching into a fishbowl.*
6. His skin *crawled.*
7. Whenever he had a migraine headache, the ticking of the clock was a *hammer* in his brain.
8. The morning after, he had a *furry* tongue.
9. His guilt clung to him like a *hair shirt.*
10. Humiliating him in his defeat was *pouring salt on his wounds.*

Exercise:
Supply appropriate figurative language to heighten the tactile effect of the following sentences.

1. His habit of not listening was a constant _____ in her side.
2. Her caress was as light as a _____ .
3. His nerves were hot _____ stretched to the breaking point.
4. That man has a keen, _____ sharp mind.
5. After he smoked, he was sure his mouth was coated with _____ .
6. The hot asphalt was like _____ beneath his feet.
7. When you bump your "crazy bone" against the wall, it feels like a thousand _____ dancing in your arm.

8. His calloused hands were like _____ on her delicate skin.

9. His unexpected proposal made her head _____.

10. The room was as hot as the inside of a _____.

The Sense of Taste

Except for *sweet, sour, salty,* and *bitter,* we have no way of describing taste except by imaginative borrowing and invention. Here are some routine attempts at expanding that basic vocabulary.

1. She devoured the *juicy* hamburger.
2. He found each chicken liver a *savory* morsel.
3. She enjoyed the *buttery* crust of the pie.
4. He found the cottage cheese too *bland.*
5. He loved *spicy* Mexican food.
6. He savored the *dryness* of the sherry.
7. She preferred the *sugary* coating to the cake inside.
8. He dearly loved *strong* coffee.
9. For him, tea was too *thin.*
10. He licked his lips at the *succulence* of the pork roast.

Exercise

Supply some descriptive words of your own to help these sentences communicate the sense of taste.

1. She liked the _____ taste of lemon on her

agreeably sour

fish.

2. His favorite cheese was a _____ cheddar.

strong

3. She preferred the _____ flavor of brick or Colby

weak

cheese.

4. They both preferred a _____ beer.

weaker

5. He woke up the next morning with a _____ taste in

bad

his mouth.

6. She complained that her mouthwash gave her _____

curative drug

breath.

7. The cake frosting had a _____ taste to it.
   <u>sickeningly sweet</u>

8. He found that cream ale had a much more_____
   <u>smooth, mature</u>
   _____ taste to it.

9. She loved the _____ taste of a kosher dill.
   <u>mouth puckering</u>

10. Tonic water has a prickly,_____ taste to it.
    <u>unsweet</u>

Occasionally we have to invent a word to describe a particular taste and simply hope that the sound and pronunciation of the word will convey the right meaning.

Example
1. Yogurt is *yummy*.
2. Undercooked french fries are *yucky*.
3. Western flapjacks are *scrumptious*.
4. Kool-aid is *blah*.
5. Jelly beans are *icky*.

Exercise
Just for fun, make up some words of your own that you think might describe, in your opinion, how the following things taste:

1. pizza   6. banana cream pie
2. oatmeal   7. fish and chips
3. cod liver oil   8. pretzels
4. sour milk   9. lunch meat
5. toothpaste   10. jello

Sometimes we use words ordinarily associated with the sense of taste to describe things not ordinarily associated with the sense of taste.

1. The old man was well known for his *vinegary* temperament.
2. She has a very *sweet* disposition.
3. He was very *bitter* about the rejection.
4. Disillusion *soured* her outlook.
5. The crowd loved her *spicy* songs.

Exercise

Supply words ordinarily associated with taste to complete these sentences.

1. The sailor had a _____ tongue as well as a _____
_____ wit.
2. The audience cringed as the pianist hit one _____
note after another.
3. Her personality was so _____, he got diabetes
just being with her.
4. He was _____ disappointed at the news.
5. How could she have the _____ to do what she
did?

Connoisseurs of wine turn the language around by using words *not* ordinarily associated with taste to describe the "indescribable" experience of imbibing their favorite beverage. Because there are so many categories of wine and so many differences within categories, wine lovers have wracked their brains (and their wineracks) to come up with a vocabulary flexible enough to suggest all the subtle variations they taste—or think they taste.

Read the following descriptions carefully and see if you can understand and possibly explain the various distinctions in taste that are being made.

1. Here is a wine with a *less cloying* taste and a more *natural, less prickly effervescence.*
2. These wines share what wine people call *charm.* That is, they are *fresh, lively, and fruity.*
3. *Charm* in a wine is an unstable virtue that can easily subside into *blandness.*
4. This wine has the *sprightliness, rich flavor, and fugitive, yet brisk underlying bitterness* for which it has always been sought.
5. This red wine is a *firmer, fuller* wine than the other.
6. Here you will find wines that are *racy and bouncy.*
7. Their appeal is *frank and immediate.*

8. These other wines are distinguished by *strength and complexity*.

9. *Velvety smoothness* cushions the impact of a *full, powerful body*.

10. Many people prefer the *power, intensity, and velvetiness* of this mature wine.

11. This *tart* white wine contains a faint trace of *salinity* that can be attributed to the sea breezes.

12. It cannot be called a *charming* wine, but at its best it has a *bracing effect* on the palate, with a *tonic, bitter aftertaste* particularly welcome when drinking it with fish.

13. Some producers are toning this down, possibly with the addition of *softer and blander* wines.

14. These wines represent the *vivacity and character* of all wines that come from this area.

15. This *dry* version is a *fine, flowery* wine, *rich* in flavor.

16. Large shippers have *flattened the character* of this exquisite wine.

17. It is an all-purpose wine—aromatic, satiny white, fragrant, *expansive and round*.

18. This is a good wine for those who like the pronounced aroma and *mouth-coating sweetness* of the muscat grape.

19. This wine has an aroma of very ripe fruit, and a *luscious, honeyed* flavor.

20. Here is a wine with more *ethereal sweetness*.

21. However, this other wine has an intenser aroma, and a *supple body* whose *sweetness* is revived by good *acidity*.

22. This wine is *powerful* but not *overbearing*.

23. It is *suave and sumptuous,* with a flavor that seldom *dries out* even in old age.

24. This wine is *softer and more delicate*.

25. It is enjoyable in its *vigorous youth* as an *engagingly grapy* wine, but it is better to wait for its maturing when it *sweeps onto the palate* with *velvety elegance* and a trail of opulent scents.

26. Here is a somewhat paler wine, *smooth, with a delicious taste of fruit and a clean, snappy finish*.

27. The result is an *intense, corpulent* wine with *huge, concentrated* flavors and high alcohol.
28. This wine has more *fruit and finesse* than others like it.
29. This is a *big, full, powerful* wine.
30. It is a wine that *envelopes the palate.*
31. With its *pronounced* flavor, it is the epitome of the *robust* Italian wine.

Exercise

Play connoisseur and see what words and phrases you can dream up to describe the tastes of one or more of the following beverages. Be inventive, imaginative, uninhibited, and original while still trying to get as close to the true taste as possible.

1. beer
2. coffee
3. iced tea
4. a soft drink
5. buttermilk
6. kool-aid
7. mineral water
8. juices
9. liqueurs
10. cocktails

The Sense of Smell

We know the odors of gas, ammonia, Limburger cheese, urine, apple blossoms, lilies of the valley, tobacco; therefore, we simply use these nouns to describe the smell or say that something else smells "like" them. However, some of the very words we use to discuss smells and the act of smelling are, themselves, suggestive of what they describe.

1. *waft:* the initial vowel sound plus the soft sound of the "f" suggest the gradual approach to the nostrils of something elusive and pleasant.
2. *pungent:* the repetition of the vowel sound plus the soft "g" and muted "n's" suggest odors rich in delicious flavor, heavy with provocative scent.
3. *aroma:* the long "o" sound between the initial and concluding "uh" sounds plus the vowel-like "r" and the humming "m"

suggest an agreeable olfactory sensation, something pungent that is gently dissipating as it is wafted through the air.

4. *stink:* the initial sound is stark, the final sound harsh and na-sal, and the short "i" is abrupt and unfriendly. To say the word, one must wrinkle one's nose as if in disgust.

5. *sniff:* the word begins harshly but concludes gently, as if it cannot make up its mind. The suggestion is one of uncer-tainty, as if the "sniff" might encounter something nice as easily as something awful.

6. *snort:* this is sniff with its mind made up. It has found the odor repulsive and is trying to reject it.

Exercise

Which words would you use in the following circumstances? Try to explain your choice.

1. The (aroma, smell, odor) of fried chicken made him even hun-grier.

2. The inspector (smelled, sniffed, snorted) around the kitchen, nosing about for evidence.

3. Try as she would, she could not quite get rid of the (stink, aroma, odor) in the sink.

4. The (stink, stench, aroma) of burning meat filled the room.

5. He took one (sniff, smell, whiff) of the polluted air and went back indoors.

6. He detected the (smell, odor, scent) of perfume in the air.

7. The room was (aromatic, pungent, odoriferous) with cigar smoke.

8. A (waft, smell, whiff) of fresh air drifted in through the win-dow.

There are, of course, many words that, by association, do appeal to the sense of smell and do make a strong impression.

Example

1. He coughed as the *acrid* smoke filled the room.

2. He recoiled when he opened the tin and discovered the *rancid* meat.
3. It was the first time he had ever been aware of the *rank* sweat of fear.
4. The soldier gagged as he stumbled over the *putrid* corpse.
5. When he walked into the smokehouse, we knew right away that the meat had turned *gamy*.

Exercise

Most words that are used to describe smells are adjectives. What adjectives would you use in the following sentences to strengthen their olfactory appeal?

1. The clothes in the attic had a _____ smell to them.
2. The room had been closed up so long, the air was _____ _____ .
3. He forgot to open the flue before lighting the fire, and for days the room smelled _____ .
4. When he peeled his tires, there was the smell of _____ _____ rubber.
5. The freshly picked vegetables still had an _____ smell to them.

Since smells are essentially indescribable, writers frequently resort to comparisons to transmit olfactory impressions.

Example
1. The furniture polish smells like fresh *lemons*.
2. The air freshener made the room smell like a *pine forest*.
3. Sulphur dioxide smells like *rotten eggs*.
4. Anti-dandruff shampoos smell like *coal tar*.
5. His after shave smells like *gasoline*.

Sometimes they try to be a bit more subtle about it.

Example
1. After the rain, the air was full of the smell of earth and bark and damp grass.

2. The attic was musty and dry and smelled of old dust and worn leather.
3. The scent of old lavender and faded roses clung to her handkerchiefs.
4. He literally reeked of soap and shampoo, starch and bleach.
5. There was a heavy, thick, sweetish smell in the air as the police raided the den.

Exercise
See if you can dig up some good olfactory words to describe the smell of the following things:

1. a geranium
2. an overripe banana
3. the interior of a new car
4. fresh laundry
5. a hospital
6. a classroom
7. the seashore
8. a gymnasium
9. cooking cauliflower
10. Limburger (or Camembert) cheese
11. an airless room
12. well-worn tennis shoes

Your senses should be sharpened by now to the versatility of this vast vocabulary of common words that can be used to add vitality to your style. Words that convey sensory impressions keep you in touch with your reader. They form the basis for figurative language (similes, metaphors, images, symbols) that invigorates the communication of ideas by involving the reader at a level of spontaneous response. As you go on with your study of style, you will see that at every turn, the sentences and paragraphs and essays that are the most readable are the ones that leave accurate and stimulating impressions.

II

Interpretations

Words depend for their meaning not only on their definitions and the associations we bring to them but also on the way we interpret them in context with other words. Therefore, although words continue to be the focal point of this section, we will necessarily become increasingly interested in what happens to them when they line up to form sentences. Sentences are the songs we play with words, but it is the words that determine whether the songs will be sour or sweet. (In this last sentence, why *songs* and not *melodies?* Would you have written this sentence in a different way? How? Why?)

Jonathan Swift defined style as "the proper word in the proper place." Today he might have said *right* or *appropriate* rather than *proper* because since his day the word *proper* has taken on the connotation of "exaggerated gentility"; and there is the danger that the definition could be interpreted as narrow and stuffy. That, of course, is not what Swift meant, and his definition, *properly* understood, is a good one. To call forth the word you want to use and fit it into the slot just waiting for it in the sentence is to know the joy of writing.

One of the areas of interpretation dealt with in this section is this business of connotation mentioned above. Words that share a common definition do not necessarily mean the same thing. If you *leave* your house, you mean one thing; if you *abandon* it, you mean something else. The Trojan Wars are *ancient* history, an authentic Chippendale is an *antique,* your grandfather is merely *old.* Motorists get *killed,* armies *slain,* rich uncles *murdered,* presidents *assassinated.* Definition, then, is only part of it; interpretation is the rest. Will the choice and position of the word evoke from the reader the interpretation you want? Did the lady *vanish, evaporate, disappear, fade,* or *dissolve?* The lady herself could, of course, easily *vanish* or *dissappear,* but only her high spirits could *evaporate* or her beauty *fade.* However, if you happen to know that she has been cast into a vat of acid, you could indeed say that she *dissolved.*

Do the children see little of their father because he is *neglectful, preoccupied, indifferent, uncaring?* All these words mean "unmindful" in a general sense, but each carries with it a subtle and separate meaning of its own that makes all the difference in what you say. These varying "connotations" are what make word choice so important. If you are careless about word choice and say *uncaring* when you mean *preoccupied,* you are in danger of (*maligning? insulting? demeaning? attacking?*) the character of the father when the truth may be that he truly does care but gets (*sidetracked? led astray? lured away? distracted?*) by other things.

Another area to be considered in this section is that of ambiguity. Some words take on double meanings when they are used in a particular context. The chorus girl accused of murder may have a hard time convincing the jury of her *innocence.* If the prosecutor accuses her of being a *one-time* hooker, does he mean that she used to do it regularly or only did it once? If she admits that she was *familiar* with the victim, how well does that mean she knew him?

Ambiguity exists when something that is intended to be taken one way can be taken in more than one way. If, however, it is the writer's intention to convey more than one meaning, he is dealing in irony, yet another matter of concern in this section. When you tell a woman who prefers tiny diamonds and designer labels that she has *simple* tastes, she may take what you say as a compliment while you may be laughing up your sleeve. If you tell a woman who designs her own clothes that they are decidedly *original*, she may think *creative* while you are thinking *eccentric*.

The key question is: Will the reader interpret what you are saying the way you want him to? If he does, then you have put the "proper word in the proper place" and are well on your way to mastering style.

4. Connotation

"The question is," said Alice, "whether you *can* make words mean so many different things."

"The question is," said Humpty Dumpty, "which is to be master—that's all."

LEWIS CARROLL
Through the Looking-Glass

Good question! Just who is master of the meanings of words? Since the first dictionary was compiled by Samuel Johnson over two hundred years ago, it has been all too easy to fall back on the dictionary as the ultimate authority and pretend to let the matter rest there. But nobody today would dream of relying on Johnson's original dictionary for anything but enjoyment and curiosity. In his day he had the last word, but the last word is only the latest word, not the ultimate word. Lexicographers don't make up meanings (although Johnson did); at best they can only record what a word means to literate people at the time the dictionary is being compiled. Even as the book is coming off the press, parts of it are becoming obsolete.

Words are like bullets. Fire one into a mattress and you get a predictable reaction. That's denotation. Fire one into a crowded auditorium and you can't be sure what reaction you will get beyond the noise. Will people freeze or panic? Will the sound echo or go dead? Will there be backfiring, ringing, reverberation? Whatever the result, that's connotation. It's the echo and backfire, the ringing and reverberation that give words their vitality.

54

It's the added meaning that ignites a word and makes it explode in several directions at once.

Take the word "clasp" as in: "She clasped him to her bosom" "Clasp" means "held," but it also means so much more— "grabbed," "pulled," "gripped," "ensnared," "clutched"; there's a feverish, desperate quality to the word that suggests strong passion, uncontrolled feeling.

Exercise

Which synonyms would you use in the following sentences? Justify your choice by trying to explain the connotations of the word.

1. The policeman (held, grabbed, pulled, gripped, ensnared, clutched) the suspect's arm and (thrust, pushed, shoved, danced, hurried, propelled) him toward the squad car.
2. The frightened woman (held, grabbed, pulled, gripped, ensnared, clutched) her purse and turned to (run away, escape, flee, get the hell out, leave, abscond).
3. During the movie she (held, grabbed, pulled, gripped, ensnared, clutched) her boyfriend's hand as the horror (mounted, intensified, continued, increased, heightened, rose, became unbearable).

When we deal in connotation, we are dealing with synonyms that share pretty much the same basic definitions. What changes, as you move from one synonym to another, is not so much the meaning but the effect. This is what makes a thesaurus a trap, for if you are unfamiliar with a certain synonym or are unsure of its usage, you may convey a connotative meaning that distorts your purpose.

See if you can figure out what is going on in this sentence:

He *infiltrated* the room, *disconsolate* over the *afflictions* he was having with algebra.

What are the connotations of the italicized words? Which words would you use in their place?

What gives a word its connotative meanings are the associations we bring to the word. The word "home" for most of us conjures up images of comfort and security, a place more warm and personal than a house or a dwelling. To a person who's never had a home it may exist as an ideal in the back of his mind. To the person far from home it means roots. But to an orphan the word "home" may mean something else entirely: an institution, something artificial, something not really his, something to run away from. Or think of "old people's home," "home for the blind," "home for unwed mothers." How does a grandmother feel when her children say to her, "Behave yourself, Gran-gran, or we'll have to put you in a home"?

What associations do you make with the following uses of the word *home?*

1. Home Sweet Home
2. Home of the Brave
3. Home on the Range
4. A house is not a home
5. home run
6. homecoming
7. home made
8. home grown
9. home style
10. home free
11. mobile home
12. nursing home

Let's say you want to choose a word to describe a person who has been less than serious about a rather serious topic. Will you call that person *arrogant, flippant, insolent, petulant?* If he is swaggering or boastful in the way he addresses the issue, you can certainly call him *arrogant,* but if he has only let his sense of humor carry him too far, he deserves no more than to be called *flippant.* If he is pompous, then his manner could be called *insolent;* but if he is peevish, then *petulant* would best describe him.

Or consider the various synonyms for the idea of "feeling sorry" about something. You might *lament* (but not *deplore*) the passing of an era while you might *deplore* (but not *lament*) the coming on of a new one. And what you *regret* is that you are powerless to prevent either.

A *modest* woman is not necessarily *timid,* a *timid* woman is not necessarily *modest,* and a *coy* one is seldom either; yet these three words are synonyms for shy and demure personality traits.

Exercise

1. If you have enough money to make ends meet, you are (affluent, prosperous, solvent).
2. If you have more than enough, you are (affluent, prosperous, solvent).
3. If you have more than you know what to do with, you are (affluent, prosperous, solvent).

Some usages are a matter of idiom. For example, there are many synonyms to express the concept of *nullification,* each of which has a distinctive connotation, but the synonym you choose is often determined solely by the person or thing being nullified. You *annul* a marriage, *cancel* a subscription, *destroy* evidence, *abolish* slavery, *revoke* a license, *repeal* a law, *reverse* a decision, *retract* a statement, *recall* an elected official, *overrule* an objection, *dissolve* parliament, *invalidate* an account. You *depose* a tyrant, *cashier* an officer, *defeat* an opponent, *unseat* a delegate, *unsaddle* a cowboy, *dethrone* a king, *defrock* (*not* disrobe!) a priest, *ungown* a professor, *disbar* a lawyer, *disbench* a judge.

Exercise (idiomatic connotations of relieve)

1. Only beautiful music will (alleviate, allay, assuage, soothe, mitigate) your savage breast.
2. Commiseration will (alleviate, allay, assuage, soothe, mitigate) your grief.
3. A sincere apology will (alleviate, allay, assuage, soothe, mitigate) your wrath.
4. Reassurances will (alleviate, allay, assuage, soothe, mitigate) your fears.
5. A surprise inheritance will (alleviate, allay, assuage, soothe, mitigate) your financial strain.

In most cases, the choice is not so easy—nor would we really want it to be. Too many idiomatic expressions make your writing sound imitative and flat. A personal style emerges when you can choose from among a variety of connotations that word which, while remaining true to the facts, is equally faithful to your feelings and to the predicted response of the reader.

Exercise

In the following sentences, choose a word from the list (or one of your own) that connotes the meaning *you think* the sentence ought to convey. Defend your choice by explaining the circumstances (you may have to be inventive here) and by identifying your feelings and what you think those of the reader should be. In doing so you may have to explain what is "wrong" with the other choices, at least as far as you are concerned. In most cases, there are no really right or wrong choices, but some will be better than others, and one is right for you.

For example: One way to (spend, pass, waste, kill) time on a long flight is to watch the movie.

Use *spend* if you want to be positive, *pass* if there is nothing better to do, *waste* if you think the time could be put to better use, *kill* if there is no way at all the time could be put to good use.

1. His body responded to the (hammering, pulsating, beating, throbbing) rhythms of the rock music.
2. The vultures swooped down and (ate, consumed, devoured, wolfed, gobbled) the carcasses of the animals.
3. They said that Ralph was guilty of (overlooking, forgetting, ignoring, neglecting) his duties as chairman.
4. The dean of the college was called in by the president and summarily (fired, dismissed, let go, canned).
5. Because of her outstanding achievements, Miss Roland (achieved, acquired, gained, attained, won, earned) the respect of all her co-workers.
6. It was such a horrible accident that she simply (erased, oblit-

erated, annihilated, wiped out) every memory of it from her mind.

7. The manager blamed the blackout on a power outage and (deplored, regretted, lamented, felt sorry about) any inconvenience to the customers.

8. In order to attract birds, the boy (circulated, spread, strewed, scattered) sunflower seeds on the ground.

9. She decided to take more courses in order to (reform, redeem, better, improve) herself.

10. Most Americans are (bothered, annoyed, disturbed, troubled) by the situation in the Middle East.

11. The Senator claimed that an investigation of his financial holdings was an attempt to (humiliate, disgrace, mortify, degrade) him in the eyes of his constituents.

12. Before she died, the victim tried to (write, scratch, scribble, scrawl) a message on the note pad.

13. When she heard the gunshot, she (leaped, jumped, rose, sprang) from her chair.

14. He had the (odd, strange, weird, peculiar, queer) habit of wearing his glasses upside down.

15. The (din, clamor, clatter, noise, racket, hubbub) of the motorcycles was deafening.

16. Looking straight ahead, she (charged, stole, crept, walked, strode, marched) across the lobby.

17. The baby (fidgeted, squirmed, wriggled, writhed) in its father's arms.

18. After a dreary week of solitude, he (heralded, acclaimed, welcomed, applauded) the arrival of his friends.

19. Knowing it was his duty, he (committed, pledged, resigned, dedicated) himself to the defense of his country.

20. A (bunch, pack, crowd, mob, group, assemblage, gathering, congregation) of angry workers stormed the foreman's shack.

21. Try as he could, he could never quite (remember, recollect, recall, call to mind) the name of the girl he had taken to the prom.

22. When it comes to making accusations in writing, it is wise to be (reticent, secretive, taciturn, terse, laconic).

23. Although he loved her dearly, he had to admit that his wife was (fat, fleshy, plump, chubby, obese, corpulent, stout).

24. Yielding to temptation was his only (fault, failing, foible, weakness, vice).

25. The boss's constant talk about finding a new assistant was obviously an attempt to (frighten, alarm, terrify, scare, intimidate) the one he had.

26. When they saw the pilot bail out, the passengers became (frightened, alarmed, terrified, scared, intimidated).

27. I (hate, abhor, detest, loathe, abominate, scorn) people who don't keep their word.

28. The rape victim said that she found the whole episode a (horrible, dreadful, fearful, ghastly, terrible) experience.

29. The judge tried to find traces of remorse in the face of the accused, but the defendant remained (mysterious, inscrutable, enigmatic, obscure, impenetrable).

30. The surgeon insisted that a reliable anesthesiologist was the one absolutely (necessary, essential, indispensable, requisite) member of his surgical team.

31. The man is so obnoxious that I find it exceedingly difficult to be (polite, courteous, civil, affable) to him.

32. We should (revere, worship, venerate, adore) those who have aged with dignity.

33. The leader of the group (expected, required, demanded, counted on) unqualified loyalty from all members of the group.

34. Angrily he picked up the expensive lighter and (threw, cast, dropped, tossed, pitched, hurled) it into the wastebasket.

35. To kiss and tell is a (mean, cheap, tacky, low, sick) thing to do.

36. In matters of charity, Scrooge was (thrifty, frugal, stingy, miserly).

37. People who live on fixed incomes have to be (cheap, thrifty, stingy, frugal).
38. In her fear, she ran to the car and (pried, wrenched, forced, yanked, pulled) the door open.
39. To foil the shoplifter, the jewelry salesman spun around and (pushed, slammed, slid, forced) the display case shut.
40. When they asked him why he had not added up the last column, the accountant replied that it was merely (a mistake, a blunder, a slip-up, an oversight, a boo-boo) on his part.

Exercise

In the spaces left blank in the following paragraph, insert the words that you think best fit the context.

Nowhere in the Caribbean is there a spot more _____ _____, a place more bereft of the _____ for human habitation than the island of Caicas Cay in the Bahamas. Windswept and curiously arid, this _____ chunk of rock _____ in the Atlantic Ocean about 150 miles off the Florida coast has no fresh water, no beach, and _____ _____ no vegetation. Only a small boat can _____ _____ near enough to the island to _____ passengers who, once they _____ are _____ immediately by _____, black flies that no repellent can _____. It is _____ that Bahamian convicts _____ death over exile to Caicas Cay.

The following paragraph is embarrassingly overwritten. Change the italicized words (and anything else necessary) to soften the shrill tone and correct other lapses in word usage.

It was a *terrible* movie. The acting was *abominable,* the story was *putrid,* and the photography was *horrible.* The *stupid* writer who *concocted such trash* has no ear whatsoever for the *manner in which civilized people converse,* and the plot is so *gnarled* and *un-strung* that *nobody in his right mind* could ever *keep up with* it *in a million years.* Why they keep *cranking* out such *garbage* is *beyond me.* It seems they could *dispense* their time in *superlative* ways, ways that would *accumulate great gobs of* glory on the *comprehensive cinematic* industry.

This next paragraph is too tame. Considering the emotional nature of the subject matter, it relaxes rather than increases the tension. Put some starch into it by using language with more exciting connotations. In this case, changing a word here and there will not be enough; you may have to rewrite the entire paragraph.

Imagination can play funny tricks on you. A sound wakes you in the night and you are sure someone is in the house, walking slowly up the stairs, and you know that soon he will enter your room and get you. Your heart beats fast, and you are frightened and uncertain about what to do. You tell yourself it is only your imagination, but that doesn't calm you. You are nervous and worried, and you know you should speak out or do something, but all you can do is wait and hope the sound will not return.

What's in a word? As you can see, just about everything. So keep a dictionary handy—and a thesaurus—but most of all keep your ear tuned to those nuances that distinguish one synonym from another and widen the range of your connotative vocabulary. Always be careful, however, not to pick synonyms at random. If you can't "sense" the difference between *acerbic* and *contentious, asperity* and *acrimony, obduracy* and *truculence,* don't just pick one out of a hat. Wait until you feel comfortable with a word before you use it. Some words you will never feel comfortable with. Don't worry about it. Let somebody else have them. There are still plenty left that you can call your own.

5. Ambiguity

Ambiguity is the cause of more misunderstanding than any other quirk of language. When we say that something is ambiguous, we mean that it is susceptible of multiple interpretations. Because English is not an inflected language (word endings do not indicate case), it is highly vulnerable to ambiguity. The position of each word in the sentence is of the utmost importance in a language in which individual words do not themselves indicate their relationship to each other. In fact, confused word order is the primary cause of ambiguity in English. It is followed by faulty reference, misleading words and phrases, and contradiction.

Word Order

The position and arrangement of words and phrases in a sentence can drastically alter the meaning of that sentence. If the words and phrases are not where they should be, meaning can become distorted and confused.

Example
1. He told her he would be there the moment she called. (Will he be two places at once?)

The sentence should read: The moment she called, he told her he would be there.

2. He smiled when he learned that she was to get the prize from someone else. (Did he learn it from someone else, or is she to get the prize from someone else?)

The sentence should read: He smiled when he learned from someone else that she was to get the prize. Or: He smiled when he learned that someone else was to give her the prize.

3. He learned of the escape through the grapevine. (Did someone escape through a grapevine?)

The sentence should read: He learned through the grapevine of the escape.

4. He came to the university with a reputation to uphold. (His reputation or the university's?)

The sentence should read: He had a reputation to uphold when he came to the university. Or: He came to a university that had a reputation to uphold.

5. There was no evidence of a cover-up of wrong-doing in the executive wing. (What *was* supposed to be going on in the executive wing, a cover-up? or wrongdoing?)

The sentence should read: There was no evidence that the executive wing covered up any wrongdoing. Or: There was no evidence that any wrongdoing in the executive wing had been covered up.

6. We almost ran into him every time we went to the drive-in. (Almost ran or almost every time?)

The sentence should read: Almost every time we went to the drive-in we ran into him.

7. He felt subconsciously that Iago was more jealous than Othello. (He felt subconsciously or Iago envied subconsciously?)

The sentence should read: He felt that subconsciously Iago was more jealous than Othello.

8. I intended to phone you often but never did. (Never phoned often or never phoned at all?)

The sentence should read: I often intended to phone you but never did.

9. I found the keys to the car which I had lost the day before. (What's lost, the keys or the car?)
The sentence should read: I found the car keys which I had lost the day before.

10. There will be a lecture tomorrow about rape in the auditorium. (What's going on in the auditorium, lecture or rape?)
The sentence should read: Tomorrow there will be a lecture in the auditorium about rape.

Exercise
Rewrite the following sentences to eliminate the ambiguity:

1. He agreed on the way to work to give me a lift. _____

2. She was so mad she forgot what she was going to say when she ran into him. _____

3. He wondered if he should visit her sometimes, but he never got around to it. _____

4. He knew secretly that she wanted him. _____

5. I saw the strangest thing I've ever seen at the mall the other day. _____

6. I thought it was a good idea yesterday. _____

7. He carried the box with the gun in his hand. _____

8. He told her he loved her while they were in the garden. _____

9. She was embarrassed to be seen driving to the supermarket in her curlers. _____

10. He told the truth to the judge on the witness stand. _____

Faulty Reference

When a pronoun does not clearly refer to an antecedent noun, the meaning of the sentence can be ambiguous.

Example

1. Bob's father died when he was twenty. (Who was twenty, Bob or his father?)
   The sentence should read: Bob was twenty when his father died. Or: Bob's father was twenty when he died. Or: Bob's father was twenty when Bob died.
2. When my mother got home from the hospital with my sister, we took pictures of her. (Of whom, the mother or the sister? The sentence should read: We took pictures of my sister when my mother brought her home from the hospital.
3. Children like comedians because they have a sense of humor. (Who has a sense of humor, the children or the comedians?)
   The sentence should read: Because comedians have a sense of humor, children like them. Or: Because children have a sense of humor, they like comedians.
4. The Smiths avoid the Joneses because they think they are better than everybody else. (Who thinks who's better?)
   This sentence can be interpreted in a number of ways. If the meaning is that the Smiths think that the Joneses consider themselves superior, and this is the Smiths' reason for avoiding them, then the sentence should read: The Smiths avoid the Joneses because the Smiths think the Joneses consider themselves superior.
5. When my ring blocked the circulation in my finger and it turned black, they told me they were afraid they'd have to cut it off. (Cut what off, the ring or the finger?)
   Probably the ring, but to leave no doubt, the sentence should read: When my ring blocked the circulation in my finger, and my finger turned black, they told me they were afraid they'd have to cut the ring off.

Exercise

Rewrite the following sentences in a way that clarifies the pronoun reference and removes the ambiguity:

1. The doctor handed the baby boy to the father with a smile on his face. _____

_____

2. A teacher would never scold a student unless he was nasty.

_____

3. She had no trouble handling the boat because she was so sleek.

_____

_____

4. The committee could not look into the problem because it was too involved. _____

_____

5. When people hold strong opinions, they are often unpleasant.

_____

_____

Misleading Words and Phrases

Many words have two or more distinctly different meanings. When the meaning inferred is not the meaning implied, the result can be quite amusing. Ordinarily the intended meaning is clear enough, and it is only someone close to the edge who reads KEEP RIGHT as a moral or political imperative, KEEP LEFT as the work of pinko perverts, and YIELD as pacifist propaganda. This is the person who "shakes well" before using and does his level best to KEEP OUT OF THE REACH OF CHILDREN. He thinks a "child-resistant cap" is a funny hat you wear to ward off nasty little "child" molesters. Is it any wonder that such a person can decline a noun but never a drink?

Exercise
Some of the phrases and titles in the following list are accidentally ambiguous, some deliberately so. Determine the alternate meanings possible and explain the way they affect the interpretation of the phrase. Then decide which phrases or titles are helped and which are harmed by the ambiguity.

 1. The Mad Housewife   6. The Lives of a Cell
 2. Grasping Moneymakers   7. Developing Film Techniques
 3. Charming Snakes   8. Cheap Shots
 4. The Descent of Man   9. Making Up
 5. Understanding Mothers   10. Bound for Pleasure

Evasiveness

When we want to be evasive, noncommittal, we often resort to statements that are conveniently ambiguous. Since these statements can be interpreted in opposite ways, they are misleading and, often, unintentionally ironic. The sentences are not rewritten in the example because there is no exclusively "right" way to rewrite them. What they require is clarification of the italicized word or phrase.

Example
1. He told me that my writing is *unusual*. (What is "unusual" writing?)
2. The mother didn't know what to say when she was told that her daughter was an *exceptional* student. (Exceptionally bright? slow? naughty?)
3. Events have taken an *interesting* turn. (Up? Down? Over?)
4. I would recommend this class to *anyone who likes this sort of thing*. (You get what you deserve? You'd be crazy to take it?)
5. I think this course should be retained in the curriculum *if it can be kept from becoming monotonous*. (Which it is now?)

Exercise
Rewrite the following sentences in whatever way you feel will eliminate their ambiguity:

1. Nobody plays the piano the way you do. _____
   _____

2. Nobody looks the way you do in a bikini. _____
   _____

3. His acting is unlike anything I've ever seen. _____

_____

4. She is as sweet as any girl I know. _____

_____

5. She's a girl who would stand out in any crowd. _____

_____

6. He was the sort of professor no student could ever forget.

_____

7. He sets for others the same standards he sets for himself.

_____

8. You've certainly done all you can to handle the situation.

_____

9. Cleveland is an unforgettable city. _____

_____

10. It's the sort of city that sticks in your memory. _____

_____

Whether ambiguity is ironic or simply evasive depends entirely upon the facts, the writer, and the reader. If you think Cleveland is a great city and you intend to convince your reader of this, you will damage your argument by calling it "unforgettable" and letting it go at that. However, if you think it's a dump and know your reader will agree, then "unforgettable" takes on ironic overtones. In short, ambiguity is permissible only when it is unmistakably used for ironic effect. Otherwise, it is simply bad style.

6. Irony

Beyond its application to particular theatrical and rhetorical techniques, the term irony remains an elusive one, and much, often pointless, controversy has arisen over its exact definition. While it is true that the term is too easily misapplied to the merely surprising or unpredictable, there does exist a fairly general understanding among writers that irony is present in any statement in which two meanings are conveyed, one literal, the other intended. It is the tension between the two meanings that produces the ironic effect.

As a technique for heightening your sensitivity to words, we will concentrate in this chapter on the way word choice can turn an ordinary statement into an ironic one by means of *understatement, overstatement,* and *cross-statement.* What makes these techniques ironic is that they depend on more than what they say to make their meaning clear. Unlike ambiguity, irony leaves no doubt in the initiated mind as to what is intended. It follows that the effect is usually humorous.

Understatement

Understatement is based on the premise that "less is more." It is a sophisticated type of irony in which the speaker wants to be tactful and truthful at the same time. He may tell lies or use euphemisms to achieve this goal.

Example
1. She's not what you would call petite.
2. Although unemployment among movie actors is rising, the residents of Beverly Hills are not exactly draining their pools.
3. If American wedding cake were introduced into Europe, bakers there would not lose any sleep.
4. Since he has repeatedly perjured himself under oath, I have some doubts about his testimony at this time.
5. When I found a strange man in my wife's closet, I was tempted to draw embarrassing conclusions.
6. Ten percent is not quite what I call a lion's share of the profits.
7. When the terrorists hijacked my plane, I realized that I would have to rearrange my vacation plans.
8. He was a veteran of the recent unpleasantness in Iran.
9. When the semi veered into my lane, it gave me pause indeed.
10. She sings well, but I don't think Beverly Sills is chewing her fingernails.
11. First she tickled him under the chin with the eggbeater; then she tapped him on the head with the rolling pin.
12. A gunshot in close quarters is a most disturbing sound.
13. Lucrezia Borgia was not exactly the girl next door.
14. I am not at all happy about your threats on my life.
15. I consider the reports of my death exaggerated.
16. I find these vicious muggings in the park tedious.
17. A walk-on part is hardly what one would call an auspicious stage debut.
18. His failure in film direction has been underrated.
19. He took exception to the accusation that he was the murderer.
20. She did curious things to his libido.

Exercise
Turn the following sentences into ironic statements by understating the point.

1. I hated the movie. _____
_____

2. Her sweaters are much too tight. _____
_____

3. He'll run right into you if you don't watch out. _____
_____

4. She lets people walk all over her. _____
_____

5. He's a mean, ill-tempered slob. _____
_____

6. She talks about herself all the time. _____
_____

7. If I were you, I wouldn't drive through that part of town on
a bet. _____
_____

8. He reads nothing but trashy magazines. _____
_____

9. When she gets mad at you, she really knows how to lay you
out. _____
_____

10. She can't cook worth a darn. _____
_____

Overstatement

Exaggeration is a common way of achieving ironic effect. When
we flatter mediocrity, for example, it is easy to damn as we praise:
"Darling, you were never better!" "It's been an absolutely perfect evening!" "I simply adored her in the part!" "Never have I
been so thrilled!" If this doesn't stick, you can always rub it in:
"I don't care what they say, I thought you were superb." "You
were fantastic!--all things considered." "Who says you're not in
top form?" "Critics, schmitics--you were great!"

Overstatements like these usually are spoken and depend for
effect on voice inflection. In writing, overstatement can be made

ironic by the use of *oxymoron* (the pairing of contradictory words: orderly confusion, deafening silence, gleeful meanness, spiritless mirth).

Example
1. She was wearing an *incredibly ordinary* dress.
2. His presence was *remarkably unnoticeable* at the party.
3. The color scheme in her house is *monotonously varied*.
4. She had a *devastatingly plain* face.
5. The new math is *bewilderingly simple*.
6. My son made a *maddeningly lucid* case for borrowing the car.
7. There she was, resisting flattery with that *pompous modesty* of hers.
8. He accepted the blame with *arrogant humility*.
9. The IRS agent had a *distressingly soothing* voice.
10. He has an *astonishingly simple* mind.

Exercise
Supply exaggerated words that give the following sentences ironic effect through overstatement.

1. Such ingenuousness can only be the result of a _____ _____ pure mind.
2. I'm all for "clean," but her house is _____ clean.
3. I blushed, but I adored her. She had a _____ vulgar sense of humor.
4. Some phonies are just carbon-copy phonies, but Jake is a _____ fake.
5. He is _____ unorthodox in his treatment of people.
6. I found the so-called comedy hilariously _____.
7. He takes a delightfully _____ attitude toward the end of the world.
8. His wife was a veritable saint who smothered him with her unregenerate _____ .
9. The remake of *King Kong* was a monumental _____ at the box office.

10. Because he knew in his heart that he wasn't at fault, he was
_____ sincere in his apologies.

Cross-statement

A cross-statement is a statement that undercuts itself, either by
suggesting dubious comparisons or by retracting at the end what
has been given at the beginning. The irony of cross-statement
can be devastating because it catches the reader off guard and
keeps him off balance.

Example
1. He accepts apologies as generously as he makes them.
2. The critics' reception of his work is as generous as his feeling
   for them.
3. Muhammed Ali is as modest about his lifestyle as he is about
   his boxing.
4. The size of his income is in inverse proportion to the size of
   his ego.
5. He can write as well as he can act.
6. He earned the respect of his colleagues the way he earned
   his degree.
7. He was as eager to get out of debt as he was to get in.
8. Her clothes bear the unmistakable imprint of her own design.
9. He is as sincere about his apology as he was about his campaign promises.
10. Simon Legree was as much fun to be with as he was to work
    for.

Exercise
Finish the following sentences by adding a cross-statement that
gives the sentences an ironic twist.

1. His taste is equal to his _____
   _____ .

2. His qualifications are as rare as _____
   _____ .

3. He's as qualified to star in the picture as he is to _____
   _____ .

4. She stays at the top the same way she _____
   _____ .

5. He was no more susceptible to flattery than he was to _____
   _____ .

6. Her friends say there's no one like her--and so do her _____
   _____ .

7. She knows her own mind _____
   _____ .

8. She handles money the way she _____
   _____ .

9. His skill in writing is equalled only by his skill in _____
   _____ .

10. She looks great considering _____
    _____ .

A little irony goes a long way. Overused, it can become cloying and make the writer seem smug, waspish, cynical. In the hands of masters like Jonathan Swift or Oscar Wilde it can retain its brilliance and bite, but the rest of us are better off indulging in it sparingly lest it backfire and make us sound "cute" instead of clever. Nevertheless, practicing it is good exercise in the development of style because it makes us more keenly aware of the versatility of language and the variety of word choices available to us. It is also good to learn how to use it so that you will know when to avoid it.

III

Combinations

The marriage between "the proper word" and "the proper place" is performed within the framework of that basic unit of idea development, the sentence. "Word" and "place" operate as a team with each dependent on the other for its ultimate choice and effect. In this section we will concentrate on arranging words into sentences, on giving those sentences style, and on putting those sentences into self-contained clusters called paragraphs.

As we explore the versatility of the sentence, we will begin by listening to the "sound" of sentences just as we listened earlier to the sound of individual words. Even when we are reading silently, the ear "hears" what the eye sees, and the impact of the sentence can be enhanced or diminished depending on the sound effects used. Reading aloud, of course, is a good way to test the effect of sound on meaning. Try this one, for example:

Calmly he talked to her, carefully choosing his words for their soothing effect.

The sound of this sentence enhances the meaning because (a) there is a consistent rhythm (**calm**ly he / **talked** to her / **care**fully / **choos**ing his / **words** for their / **sooth**ing ef / **fect**)**;** and (b) there are parallel vowel sounds (c**a**lmy-t**a**lked; ch**oo**sing-s**oo**thing).

Now listen to this version:

He spoke calmly to her with words selected carefully for their comforting impact.

The sound diminishes the meaning because (a) the rhythm is jerky (He spoke **calm**ly to her / with **words** se**lec**ted **care**fully / for their **com**forting **im**pact); (b) the sounds are harsh (spo**k**e-**c**almly; sele**c**ted-**c**arefully; **c**omforting-effe**ct**); and (c) the word choice is inappropriate (selected, impact). Incidentally, if even "selected carefully" were reversed, the sound of the sentence would already be improved. It is not just the sense, then, but also the sound of a sentence that can determine the choice and position of a word.

Varieties of sentence structure are a major concern of this section. Not all parts of a sentence are equal, and there are numbers of ways of expressing the varying relationships among those parts. Take these two simple items: *The phone rang. She did not answer it.* Here are some of the ways you might combine these two items into one sentence:

The phone rang, and she did not answer it.
The phone rang, but she did not answer it.
When the phone rang, she did not answer it.
She did not answer the phone when it rang.

Add this item: *She was afraid,* and you could come up with these possibilities:

The woman, who was afraid, did not answer the phone.
Afraid to answer it, she let the phone ring.
Because she was afraid, her phone rang unanswered.
That she was afraid was the reason she did not answer the phone.

When the phone rang, she did not answer it because she was afraid.

These are some of the basic varieties of sentence structure. Once you have become familiar with them, you will be ready to experiment with constructions of a more sophisticated nature. Under sentence style you will learn how to construct *loose, balanced,* and *periodic* sentences, variations that will become important to you later on when you are learning to distinguish between, say, the plain style of writing and the grand one.

Following this you will move on to one of the most critical elements of style: *transition.* Knowing how to progress smoothly and logically from one sentence to another and from one paragraph to another is, in a way, the key to good style. Transition is the glue that holds paragraphs and essays together, and there are techniques for mastering it that no writer can afford to ignore.

Transition leads automatically into paragraphing, the concern of the last chapter of this section. There you will see that a paragraph is not just an accumulation of discrete sentences but a sequence of interrelated ones, each devoted to the same topic, each connected to whatever precedes or follows it. Here at last you will go beyond the statement of a single thought to the presentation and development of a whole idea. Since a paragraph is an essay in miniature, understanding its function and design is excellent preparation for mastering the art of the total essay.

7. Sentence Rhythm

Someone once defined poetry as good writing struggling to become prose and prose as good writing struggling to become poetry. Unhelpful as these statements may be as definitions of either poetry or prose, they do suggest a truth about both kinds of writing. A good sentence has a tempo to it, a rising and a falling, a balance and a flow, that the ear hears as the eye reads and that contributes, however subtly, to the message the sentence is communicating. An urgent message may require a faster tempo, a solemn message a more leisurely one. Whatever the message may be, the sentence that delivers it best is the one in which the sound suits the sense. What this means to you as a stylist is that, in addition to the sound effects presented in Chapter 2, you need to sharpen your sense of rhythm.

As we practice our writing by trying out various word usages and sentence patterns, we begin, quite naturally, to acquire an ear for rhythm. We begin to "feel" when repetition or redundancy or rearrangement can fine tune a sentence and give it a cadence appropriate to its content. Because rhythm is an acknowledged technique of poetry (or used to be), poets have long since developed a vocabulary for identifying varieties of rhythmic patterns. For convenience, then, we will use this vocabulary and imitate these patterns, but we will constantly bear in mind that it is prose we are writing and not poetry. Even so, in an exercise of this nature, there is bound to be a certain amount of exaggeration, a tendency to become artificial and singsongy. Such exaggeration is part of any drill, which is by nature self-conscious, and in this case it can be half the fun. There is no danger that you will go away writing poetic paragraphs. What is more likely to happen is that you will become more sensitive than you have been before to this important but neglected element of good prose style.

First, a brief review of common word rhythms:

iambic: two syllables, the first unstressed, the second stressed (to-**day**, to**night**, be**ware**, con**form**, de**light**, pre**vent**, in**spire**, be**gin**, un**nerve**, for**get**

trochaic: two syllables, the first stressed, the second unstressed (**after**, **common**, **sexy**, **silly**, **fran**tic, **has**sle, **both**er; **Thom**as, **Ste**ven, **Emma**, **Su**san—most Anglo-Saxon two-syllable names)

dactylic: three syllables, the first one stressed, the last two unstressed (**terr**ify, **ab**dicate, **in**filtrate, **ser**monize, **dig**nity; often found in word combinations—**go** for it, **stop** that man, **lis**ten now, **tick**ets please)

anapestic: three syllables, the first two unstressed, the last one stressed (conde**scend**, disbe**lief**, unde**ceive**, incor**rect**, outper-**form**; usually found in word combinations—at a **time**, in the **dark**, one or **two**, in con**tempt**, up the **wall**, down be**low**, inside **out**, upside **down**)

Iambic Rhythm

Example:
He lived in undisturbed seclusion, far away from all the troubles that had plagued his early years.
He **lived** in un**dis**turbed se**clu**sion, **far** a**way** from **all** the **troub**les **that** had **plagued** his **ear**ly **years**.

Exercise:
Underline the stressed syllables in the following sentences and
then read the sentences aloud to note the iambic rhythm.

1. A man who doesn't plan is one who sort of hopes that things
   will come his way.
2. It didn't take me long to see the boss was good and mad that
   I was late.
3. I know I shouldn't really try so hard, but if I don't, then who
   will ever get it done?
4. Today he'll tell you what he plans to do this evening, then
   tonight he'll change his mind and end up doing something
   else.
5. To see a person in distress and know that you can be of help
   is wonderful indeed.

Although you were correct if you marked every other syllable
in the preceding sentences as either stressed or unstressed in order to emphasize the iambic rhythm of the sentences, you would
never actually read the sentences that way. For example, sentence
(5) would be read like this: To **see** a person in distress and **know**
that you can be of help is **won**derful indeed. Although we have
reduced the number of stressed syllables from eleven to three, it
is owing to the underlying iambic rhythm that these syllables
that are actually stressed are spaced in such a way that the sentence pleases our ear.

Exercise
Complete the following sentences by emphasizing iambic rhythm
even though the sentences would not actually be read with such
exaggerated emphasis.

1. The **on**ly **way** to **see** the **world** _____

   _____

2. It's **all** too **ea**sy **to** for**get** _____

   _____

3. The **man** who **tries** to **hide** the **truth** _____
_____

4. Be**cause** the **door** was **left** ajar _____
_____

5. The **car** was **run**ning **very** **well** until _____
_____

Trochaic Rhythm

Example
Mark was always in a hurry, never stopping once to ponder what it was he really wanted.
Mark was **al**ways **in** a **hur**ry, **nev**er **stop**ping **once** to **pon**der **what** it **was** he **real**ly **want**ed.

Exercise
Underline the stressed syllables in the following sentences and then read the sentences aloud to note the trochaic rhythm.

1. Cowards never take a chance unless they're risking someone else's life.
2. Students who are motivated always get the higher marks in courses.
3. Simple people have a happy outlook, never letting petty problems cloud their sunny spirits.
4. Hoping to improve your writing style while doing nothing to improve your mind is simply wishful thinking.
5. Pregnant women may crave pickles in the morning for their breakfast, but they seldom feel like jogging in the evening.

Complete the following sentences by emphasizing trochaic rhythm.

1. **Mon**ey **may** not **grow** on **trees,** but _____
_____

2. **Flan**nel **night**gowns **do** a **lot** to _____
_____

3. **Woolly blankets may** do **even more** to _____

_____

4. **Eating too** much **can**dy **can** be _____

_____

5. **Drink**ers **never worry if** the **traf**fic _____

_____

Dactylic Rhythm (dum diddy, **dum** diddy)

Example
Magnified images flickered sporadically, fading then brightening
the closer they came to the mother ship.
Magnified **im**ages **flick**ered spo**rad**ically, **fad**ing then **bright**ening
the **clo**ser they **came** to the **moth**er ship.

Exercise
Underline the stressed syllables in the following sentences and
then read the sentences aloud to note the dactylic rhythm.

1. She was convinced that the manager's plan was not practical.
2. Here I am practically trapped in this godawful nursery.
3. Thoughtlessly signalling left at the corner, I turned to the right
   and ran smack into Officer Mulligan.
4. Down on the farm we grow all kinds of vegetables: cabbages,
   radishes, carrots, and cucumbers.
5. Several reporters have interviewed both of us.

Complete the following sentences by emphasizing dactylic
rhythm.

1. **Once** I was **chas**ing a **truck** down the **high**way when _____

_____

2. **Fol**lowing **close**ly be**hind** me, the **bi**cycle **sud**denly _____

_____

3. **Out** of the **al**ley with **fright**ening **speed** came a _____

_____

4. **All** I could **hear** was the **sick**ening **sound** of the _____

_____

5. **Hon**esty **may** be a **prac**tical **pol**icy **if** you are _____
_____

Anapestic Rhythm (diddy **dum**, diddy **dum**)

Example
Undeterred by the fact that his offer was quite insincere, she accepted at once.
Unde**terred** by the **fact** that his **off**er was **quite** insin**cere,** she
ac**cep**ted at **once.**

Exercise
Underline the stressed syllables in the following sentences and
then read the sentences aloud to note the anapestic rhythm.

1. In a time of distress there come heartaches that cannot be
   eased.
2. If you must discontinue that popular line, please make sure
   that our customers do understand.
3. She was most indiscreet when she let it be known that she
   once had been thrown into jail.
4. I can tell at a glance if the car has been parked near the sea.
5. Indigestion is bad if you don't know the right thing to take
   and you're left indisposed and awake with a most disagreeable, quite indescribable ache.

Complete the following sentences by emphasizing anapestic
rhythm.

1. When the **House** recon**venes** in the **fall,** _____
   _____

2. **Be**fore you a**ban**don your **house,** discon**nect** _____
   _____

3. What you **see** in be**tween** _____
   _____

4. She was **still** unpre**pared** _____
   _____

5. There are **times** when you **must** disap**point** _____
   _____

Mixed Rhythm

The following sentences begin with one rhythm pattern and then change (after the slash) to another. Without worrying too much about the names of the patterns, see if you can detect the shift in the first sentence of each pair and then complete the second sentence accordingly.

1. When you know who you are / you seldom lose your way.
   If the plane is on time / _____
2. Should it occur to you / be sure to drop a line.
   If it comes down to it / _____
3. Silly little symptoms are quite easily neglected, though, through / ignorance, carelessness, laziness, or foolishness.
   Pointless and debilitating arguments get out of hand through/
   _____
4. After the bloodthirsty, spine-chilling cry in the wilderness / we grabbed our gear and beat it back to town.
   Silently whispering, secretly wondering, all they could think of was / _____
5. Dancing cheek to cheek, the lovers never knew the moment when the music ended; / it was clear they were lost and alone in their own private world of romance.
   Clutching at the floating straw, the drowning man was frantic; _____
6. Sometime soon before the snow flies / we will jump in the car and run down to my farm in the hills.
   Later when the days are shorter and those winter nights seem endless / _____
7. A candidate for public office really has to guard his tongue; / otherwise enemies looking for weaknesses may get the best of him.
   The time to buy your Christmas gifts is early in the fall; /
   _____
8. At the sound of the bell all the children come out of the school / laughing, screaming, glad to have some time to run and play.

We had just crossed a side street when all of a sudden this car / _____

9. Once you have made up your mind to go through with it, / you will not have the chance to go back on your word.
Big juicy hamburgers, crisp golden french-fries and thick chocolate malteds / _____

10. Every time I open up my paycheck, / I get red in the face at the paltry amount that I find in there.
Sordid stories made their rounds among the neighbors / _____
_____

Although you are not expected to tap your foot or have a metronome handy while you are writing an essay, you will be wise to pay more attention to prose rhythm than you probably have been. When you don't like what you have written and you're not sure just what it is that's wrong, read it aloud and listen to the sounds and the rhythms. You will be surprised at how often you can improve the quality of a sentence by merely transposing a few words here and there or rearranging the position of clauses or phrases. It's very likely that, as you read and listen, you will "hear" words begging to be deleted and others begging to take their place. You may not always write with rhythm on your mind, but it doesn't hurt to revise with rhythm in mind.

8. Sentence Structure

Dick and Jane go to college. They go to Bowling Green. Bowling Green is a large state university. It is in Ohio. Dick and Jane are learning sentence combining. It is a new way of teaching sentence structure. They have found it helpful. It has helped their writing very much.

Run that by me again.

Dick and Jane, who attend Bowling Green, a large state university in Ohio, have found that sentence combining, a new way of teaching sentence structure, has helped their writing very much.

As you can see, the sentence above is a synthesis of the seven short sentences in the opening paragraph. If they both say the same thing, why is it that we prefer the one long sentence to the seven short ones? Perhaps they don't really say the same thing after all. They both convey the same information, but there is a difference in emphasis. When you read the seven short sentences, you don't know what is important and what is not. You don't know what point the writer is trying to make. That both Dick and Jane attend Bowling Green is given the same emphasis as the fact that they are both learning sentence combining or that sentence combining is a new way of teaching sentence structure or that sentence combining has helped them in their writing.

The need for balancing major and minor ideas within the same sentence does not have to be labored. Most of us found the monotony of the opening paragraph intolerable even in the first grade. By now it seems simple-minded and insulting. In fact, it takes an effort to reduce a decent idea to its component parts and place each within its own little sentence. However, it's a well-known fact that you have to take something apart first before you can put it back together in a different form.

Sentence combining, which is a highly effective way of learning the varieties of syntactical options, begins with the reduction of complex ideas to their simplest parts. These parts are then written out in a string of short, simple sentences. Your task is to take these parts and blend them into one good, workable, readable sentence. When you have practiced combining sentences according to a variety of structural techniques, you will be much more aware of the possibilities available to you when you come to write original prose.

It is easy to fall into lazy syntactical habits, either because we can't be bothered to try other options or because we are unfamiliar or uncomfortable with other options. Once you have worked your way carefully through the eight major sentence combining techniques in this chapter, you will find yourself experimenting more boldly with ways of expressing your own thoughts. Never lose sight of the fact that the way you say something is fully as important as what you have to say.

Coordination

Coordination is the technique of combining simple sentences by the use of conjunctions that give each sentence (independent clause) equal weight. The coordinating conjunctions are: and, but, or, nor, for, yet, so. (*So* is still frowned upon in some quarters, but modern usage allows it.) Here is how coordination works:

Example

1. The student has a problem. He should consult his instructor.
   The student has a problem, *and* he should consult his instructor.
2. The student has a problem. He refuses to consult his instructor.
   The student has a problem, *but* he refuses to consult his instructor.
3. The student has a problem. He refuses to consult his instructor. He does not want to admit that anything is wrong.
   The student has a problem, *but* he refuses to consult his instructor, *for* he does not want to admit that anything is wrong.

Identify the coordination in the following sentence combinations:

1. The technical operation of this activity is highly complex, yet these vessels have achieved a remarkable level of success.
2. Boring in running seas can be extremely difficult, and in really heavy weather operations may have to be suspended.
3. In normal conditions it is extremely effective, but like the discovery ships it has its drawbacks.
4. He did not contest the charge, nor did he admit guilt, for he alone knew the truth of the matter, and he was sworn to secrecy.
5. There was no use hanging around just waiting to be thrown out, so he grabbed his gear and took off.

Exercise

Combine the following sentences by means of coordination:

1. I asked him to move. He refused to budge. _____
   _____

2. You may have it picked up. You may bring it in. _____
   _____

3. You have to buy a used car with caution. It is all too easy to be taken in by an unscrupulous salesman. _____
   _____
   _____

4. Jack wants to go. Jill wants to go. Jerry doesn't want to have any part of it. _____

_____

5. The food is good. The drinks are lousy. Bring your own bottle.

_____

_____

Subordination

Subordination is the technique of combining sentences by using conjunctions which turn one sentence into a *dependent clause*. Some common subordinating conjunctions are: if, when, whenever, since, as, because, although, whereas, where, before, after. They are easy to spot because they either set up an expectation that is satisfied in the independent clause, or they qualify information included in a preceding independent clause.

Example
1. I watch television. I fall asleep.
   Whenever I watch television, I fall asleep.
2. I cannot work. There is too much noise.
   I cannot work *because* there is too much noise.

Identify the use of subordination in the following sentence combinations:

1. I've signed up to take the test tomorrow although I'm not really sure I'm ready.
2. She resumed reading where she had left off.
3. As I was going down the stair, I met a man who wasn't there.
4. While there's life in you, spread your wings and fly.
5. I want to squeeze all I can out of life before the parade passes by.

Exercise
Combine the following sentences by means of subordination:

1. The children loved the trip. There was always something going on. _____

_____

2. You haven't tried it. Don't knock it. _____

_____

3. I was walking across the campus. I saw a most unusual sight.

_____

_____

4. Her character was above reproach. His had serious defects.

_____

5. He is very elusive. I still intend to track him down. _____

_____

Relative Clauses

A relative clause is a dependent clause that is related to a particular noun in an independent clause by means of a *relative pronoun* (who, whom, whose, which, that).

Example
1. The candidate got the job. He was the last to apply.
   The candidate *who was the last to apply* got the job.
2. The woman has filed a complaint. Her purse was snatched.
   The woman *whose purse was snatched* filed a complaint.
3. That gunk is really honey. It looks like wax.
   That gunk, *which looks like wax,* is really honey.

Identify the relative clauses in the following combinations:

1. I don't trust the man who is sitting in the third seat from the left.
2. The student whom everyone wanted for the office declined to run.
3. The money that I had carefully saved for a vacation went to pay the medical bills.
4. A certain singer whose name is a household word has threatened the life of this columnist.
5. I like fireworks that really light up the sky.

Exercise

Combine the following sentences by turning one into a relative clause and inserting it in the proper place:

1. This wine is excellent with fish. It should be served chilled.

   _____

2. The man has turned himself in. He masterminded the heist.

   _____

3. The students suffer. They don't cheat. _____

   _____

4. This problem will not be solved easily. It has been around for a long time. _____

   _____

5. The program will not be shown this evening. It is regularly scheduled at this time. _____

   _____

Participial Phrases

A participial phrase is used when you want to compress two sentences that have the same subject into one. You do this by dropping the subject from one of the sentences and using only the present or the past participle of the verb.

Example
1. He ran across the field. He was waving his arms frantically.
   He ran across the field, *waving his arms frantically.*
2. He was denied entrance to the building. He stomped off in a rage.
   Denied entrance to the building, he stomped off in a rage.
3. He was forgotten by his friends. He had difficulty keeping up his spirits.
   Forgotten by his friends, he had difficulty keeping up his spirits.

Identify the participial phrases in the following sentence combinations:

1. Angered by the attack, the animal fought back.
2. He withdrew into himself, discouraged by all he had seen.
3. Cheered by the good news, the girl fairly danced down the street.
4. They ran down the stairs, laughing all the way.
5. He sat on the curb, sickened by the sight, wondering when the fighting would ever end.

Exercise
Combine the following sentences by turning one of them into a participial phrase:

1. She was overcome by emotion. She burst into tears. _____
   _____

2. She was embittered by the experience. She resolved never to do it again. _____
   _____

3. He was in agony. He was torn by desires he did not understand. _____
   _____

4. He thought no one would notice. He fell asleep. _____
   _____

5. She walked rapidly. She wondered if anyone was following her. She didn't see the dark shape in the doorway. _____
   _____

Appositives

Appositives are phrases inserted into a sentence in order to define or identify something. They are time-saving abbreviations of what would otherwise be a cumbersome series of simple sentences all having the same subject.

Example
1. O. P. Yum is in town. O. P. Yum is my favorite country singer.
   O. P. Yum, *my favorite country singer,* is in town.

2. Watertower Place has everything. It is a high-rise mall in Chicago.
Watertower Place, *a high-rise mall in Chicago,* has everything.

Identify the appositives in the following sentence combinations:

1. *The Godfather,* the biggest selling paperback book in publishing history, is about the Mafia.
2. Love, a frequently misunderstood emotion, is a many-splendored thing.
3. The winner, a young man with charm and talent, has everything going for him.
4. They turned the lights back on in the city, a city that had been blacked out for five years.
5. Many famous comedians—men like Bob Hope, George Burns, Jack Benny—got their start in vaudeville.

Exercise
Combine the following sentences by turning one of them into an appositive and inserting it in the appropriate place.

1. Dr. Spex is a great guy. He is my eye doctor. _____
   _____

2. Elvis Presley became a legend in his own time. He was a country-rock singer from Memphis. _____
   _____
   _____

3. Cincinnati is a sprawling city on the banks of the Ohio River. It is the home of the Reds. _____
   _____
   _____

4. We were forced to eat all kinds of food. It was food you couldn't have paid us to eat back home. _____
   _____
   _____

5. Some of America's largest states have the smallest populations. One thinks of states like Montana, Wyoming, Utah, and

Nevada. _____

_____

_____

Absolutes

An absolute is a simple sentence that is subordinated to an independent clause by removing or altering its verb form to establish a closer connection between clauses.

Example
1. verb removed entirely:
   The girl stood up to speak. Her heart *was* in her throat.
   The girl stood up to speak, *her heart in her throat.*
2. auxiliary verb removed:
   He looked across the table at it. His mouth *was* watering for the first taste.
   He looked across the table at it, *his mouth watering for the first taste.*
3. verb changed to present participle:
   Suddenly he shifted position. His legs *tensed.* His stomach tightened with excitement.
   Suddenly he shifted position, *his legs tensing, his stomach tightening with excitement.*

Identify the absolutes in the following sentence combinations.

1. He crouched in the corner of the car, his face a mask of fear.
2. His throat constricted with apprehension, he ventured the crucial question.
3. Its glass shattered, its body rusted, its tires worn, the car was little more than a pile of junk.
4. The bloodhounds yapping at her rear-end, Eliza fled across the frozen river.
5. The student was on the edge of his seat, pencil poised, eager for the test to begin.

Exercise
Combine the following simple sentences by using absolutes.

1. His house was trashed by vandals. He vowed revenge. _____

2. The tall man strode across the room. His head almost scraped the ceiling. _____

3. He could see it all in a flash. His friends were deserting him. His wife was leaving him. His future was going down the drain. _____

4. The room was a mess. Cigarette butts were heaped in the ash-trays. Stuff was spilled all over the floor. Chairs and tables were overturned. Cups and plates were everywhere. _____

5. His vision was beginning to blur. He was afraid he would have to pull off to the side of the road and sleep. _____

Noun Substitutes

A noun substitute is a simple sentence that has been converted into a noun clause by beginning the sentence with either the word "that" or an altered form of the verb.

Example
1. You will be here. It makes me happy.
   That you will be here makes me happy.
2. They begged for mercy. It did them no good.
   Begging for mercy did them no good.

3. One should not belch at the table. It is bad manners.
   To belch at the table is bad manners.

Identify the noun substitutes in the following sentence combinations.

1. Losing one's way is a frightening thing.
2. That I miss you goes without saying.
3. That life is a comedy of errors is sometimes too true to be comic.
4. To finish one's day's work is not always easy.
5. Driving while intoxicated is criminal.

Exercise
Combine the following sentences by turning one of them into a noun substitute.

1. You don't like me. It makes me sad. _____
   _____

2. We drove along country roads. It was great fun. _____
   _____

3. I take pictures. It is my hobby. _____
   _____

4. You do a job right. It is very satisfying. _____
   _____

5. One takes precautions. It is a wise thing to do. _____
   _____

Rearrangement

Rearrangement is the technique of combining sentences so as to place the emphasis where it will get the best response from the reader. Traditionally, the end of the sentences is considered to be the most emphatic part, the beginning less emphatic, and the middle least.

Example

1. New England weather is unpredictable.
   That is what we were told.
   We were in Boston.

   a. We were told, while we were in Boston, that New England weather is unpredictable.
   b. While we were in Boston, we were told that New England weather is unpredictable.
   c. That New England weather is unpredictable is what we were told while we were in Boston.

2. There is a rumor among the wags of Washington.
   They say the first lady has plans to paint the White House.
   They say she plans to paint it pink.

   a. It is being rumored among the wags of Washington that the first lady has plans to paint the White House pink.
   b. Among the wags of Washington it is being rumored that the first lady has plans to paint the White House pink.
   c. That the first lady has plans to paint the White House pink is what is being rumored among the wags of Washington.

Exercise

Combine these sentences three ways giving each one its turn at the end; then decide on which you think is most effective.

1. He was awakened.
   There was a rattling at the window.
   It was the middle of the night.

   a. _____
   b. _____
   c. _____

2. He would never walk again.
   It was sad news.
   The doctor had to tell him.

   a. _____

b. _____

c. _____

3. A murder was plotted.
   The wife did it.
   The husband did not do it.

   a. _____

   b. _____

   c. _____

4. There was a murderer.
   He was Alfred Quint.
   He was the man we least suspected.

   a. _____

   b. _____

   c. _____

There is no formula for putting sentence variety to work. No one actually says to himself, "I'll begin with a simple sentence, follow it with a compound one, then use subordination in the third, a participial phrase in the fourth, an absolute in the fifth, and wind it up with a noun substitute in the sixth." However, there's nothing wrong with being a little self-conscious about trying out various structures when you are in the process of enlarging your syntactical repertoire and upgrading your style. Before you plunge into that second or third sentence, take time out to review the options available to you; then try out a few before you make your final choice. If you're deliberate now, you'll be spontaneous later.

9. Sentence Style

Beyond the varieties of syntactical constructions presented in the previous chapter there are three basic stylistic options available to the writer. The most common of these is the *loose* sentence. One way to define a *loose* sentence would be to say that it is simply any sentence that is neither *periodic* nor *balanced*. A less negative definition identifies a *loose* sentence as one that is put together like a freight train, section by section, with parts that can be separated and removed without damage to the meaning. Whereas *periodic* and *balanced* sentences are orchestrated so that they must be read in their entirety to be understood, a *loose* sentence is an add-on sentence, written piecemeal, so to speak, as additional thoughts occur to the writer.

Example
We had a bad winter, and now we're having a wet summer, so it's hard to know just what is happening to the weather, but there are those who say the climate is changing and that we're in for worse weather for the rest of the century.

Notice how the sentence just chugs along, one item following another in almost random fashion, resulting in a succession of clauses connected by coordinating conjunctions. There is a slackness to a *loose* sentence, a lack of tension. There is no real build-up, no anticipation, no excitement. Loose sentences are comfortable sentences, and they work very nicely within a long essay as islands of relaxation between more tensely structured sentences. Unless you are already a polished stylist, loose sentences are fairly easy to write because they seem almost to lack style. They don't, of course, because you can easily get lost when you allow yourself to ramble, but they are hardly sentences that require lengthy or complicated instruction.

Exercise
Combine the following simple sentences into one *loose* sentence:

1. I like breakfast.
2. I like dinner.
3. I don't like lunch.
4. I don't think I'll have anything right now.
5. You go ahead and order something.
6. Don't worry about me.

_____

_____

_____

_____

If you're not exactly sure what a *loose* sentence is, you'll get a better idea once you have gone through the exercises on *periodic* and *balanced* sentences.

Periodic sentences

A periodic sentence is a tightly structured sentence that waits until the last word or phrase to make its point. In this way, the sentence tension builds as preliminary information piles up. Since the clincher is withheld until the last moment, there is no way that the sentence can make sense until the period at the end has been reached. This is why it is called a *periodic* sentence. It is probably the most formal and sophisticated sentence structure possible, and it has been used to great effect by fine writers past and present. Because it is so carefully structured, however, so "stylized," it has to be used with skill and caution. Used wisely, a *periodic* sentence can add the excitement of suspense to your writing and keep your readers interested in going on by arousing their curiosity.

Example

1. Unless we close ranks, pull together, and rededicate ourselves to our noble cause, we shall never maintain our freedom.
2. Hollow with fear, the little man carefully locked the door behind him, pulled down the shades, and then nervously opened the desk drawer and drew out the girlie magazine.
3. Care of the aged, protection of the wrongly accused, relief for the suffering, security for the poor, these were the issues that he thought the press exaggerated.
4. That you are never here when you are supposed to be or never prepared to recite when you are here is a defect in your character that I intend to exploit.
5. One of my greatest concerns is that the leadership of the world is in the hands of those who are likely to do the job poorly.
6. Her sudden fame, her astronomical rise to stardom, and, even more than that, her ability to stay at the top are elements of a career that, to me, will always remain a mystery.
7. It was not until I saw her standing there on the platform, a band around her hair, glasses slipping down her nose, feet squeezed into tight little boots, that I wondered how I had failed to find her charming.
8. The intensity of his interest, the enormousness of his concern, and the brilliance of his reasoning were the things that, in the end, betrayed him.
9. Not until all avenues have been explored, all stones unturned, all cupboards ransacked, will we be able to rest.
10. Given the nature of his work—the effort with which he goes about it, the pain with which he does it, the predictability of its outcome—is it any wonder that he has consistently failed?

Exercise

Finish these sentences in *periodic* style:

1. Not until we take responsibility for the underprivileged _____

2. Unless we take the bull by the horns _____

3. That he cannot attend the meeting _____

4. Given his taste for good living _____

5. Trembling with delight, the girl _____

6. Regard for human rights, respect for human dignity _____

7. What bothers me most _____

8. His habits, his routine, his needs _____

9. It is only a matter of time _____

10. Situated as it is in the center of the city _____

Balanced Sentences

Balanced sentences are sentences that are constructed according to the principles of *parallel structure, antithesis,* or *symmetry.* In each case, a pattern that has been established at the beginning of the sentence is repeated elsewhere in the sentence. Balance tightens the structure of a sentence but does not make it quite so tense as a *periodic* sentence. Note that a *balanced* sentence may be *periodic* but is not necessarily so. (There were parallel structures in many of the examples given under *periodic* sentences.)

Parallel Structure

Parallel structure is the setting up of a series of nouns, verbs, phrases, clauses, or sentences.

Example
1. (nouns) Liberty, equality, fraternity—these were the avowed principles of the French Revolution.
2. (verbs) I will love, honor, and obey her.
3. (phrases) I longed to rush to her, to hold her in my arms, to comfort her.
4. (clauses) Give me a man who will think before he questions, who will question before he decides, who will decide before it's too late.
5. (sentences) I dislike a man who disgraces a public office. I dislike the people who let him stay in office. I dislike myself for standing by and letting it happen.

Parallel structure can particularize a generality:
1. Nobody could come to the party: Jake had to work, George had to study, and Jerry had to go somewhere else.
2. I never saw such a hectic scene: ambulances clogging the street, policemen holding back the crowd, onlookers craning to catch a glimpse of the accident, victims crying for help.

Parallel structure can heighten an emotional effect:
1. When I think of unwanted children, my heart aches; when I see lonely old people, my soul suffers; when I encounter the sick and the destitute, my throat constricts; when I consider all the injustice in the world, my blood boils.
2. When I first heard about it, I was upset; when I then saw it, I was angry; when I now stop to think about it, I am outraged.

Exercise
Using parallel structure, construct sentences employing the type of series indicated in parentheses.

1. (nouns) _____

_____

2. (verbs) _____

_____

3. (phrases) _____

_____

4. (clauses) _____

_____

5. (sentences) _____

_____

Antithesis

Antithesis is the technique of pitting one half of a sentence against the other. Sentences of this kind are usually wise or witty (or try to be) and usually appear as *aphorisms*.

Example
1. He hoped for the best but prepared for the worst.
2. The sins we commit are the ones we are often quickest to condemn.
3. Money doesn't buy happiness, but it's easy to be unhappy without it.
4. Sins are committed in ecstasy and concealed in despair.
5. We are too quick to beg forgiveness and too slow to bestow it.
6. The less sure a man is of what he believes, the harder he will try to get you to agree with him.
7. The only way to overcome temptation is to yield to it. (Oscar Wilde)
8. The more some people are satisfied, the more they gripe.
9. Many things that are hard to explain are easy to understand.
10. He preserved his virtue by keeping a constant watch on vice.

Exercise
Complete the following "aphorisms" by using *antithesis* to give the sentences *balance*. Some of the sayings will be familiar to you.

1. The spirit is willing, _____

_____

2. Marry in haste; _____

_____

3. The first to praise you _____

_____

4. Sometimes the activity which promises least _____

_____

5. A man who is blind to his own shortcomings _____

_____

6. It is one thing to fantasize _____

_____

7. A person who is easy on himself _____

_____

8. Promises are easily made _____

_____

9. The person you can't live without today _____

_____

10. Easy come, _____

_____

Symmetry

The technique of achieving balance in a sentence by means of symmetry is to invert the second of two parallel structures. (The rhetorical term for such inversion is *chiasmus*.) As with antithesis, the result is often *aphoristic*.

Example
1. Maybe he wasn't the best teacher we ever had, but then we weren't the best class he ever had.
2. Do we exist to serve the government, or does the government exist to serve us?
3. Don't ask how you can preserve your own interests but how your own interests can preserve you.
4. It wasn't the best wine I ever tasted, but then I haven't tasted all that much wine.
5. If it's good to deny evil, it's also evil to deny good.

6. Some people hear with what they sit on while others sit on everything they hear.
7. We could not love God if God did not love us.
8. We would not need God if God did not need us.
9. Don't tell me what I can do for posterity; tell me what posterity has ever done for me.
10. People worry too much about forgetting to be able to forget their worries.

Exercise
Complete the following sentences by using *symmetry* to give the sentence *balance*. Some of the expressions may be familiar to you.

1. Winners never quit; _____
   _____

2. Some people eat to live; others _____
   _____

3. If you're not with the one you love, _____
   _____

4. Some work at play while others _____
   _____

5. Don't ask what society can do for you, _____
   _____

6. If you can't have the job you like, _____
   _____

7. How you keep up with company depends _____
   _____

8. A lady who lives to love, _____
   _____

9. Drivers shouldn't drink, and _____
   _____

10. If you itch to start from scratch, _____
    _____

Turn the following sentences into either *periodic* or *balanced* ones:

1. So many unprepared people are flooding the job market. This is one of our worst social problems. Something has to be done about it.
2. Freedom is a word that is talked about a lot and used at every turn to sanctify a sentiment, but nobody has ever yet adequately defined it.
3. Her guilt was obvious to all of them. The police were sure of it. The spectators sensed it. The jury was ready to pronounce it. The judge was convinced of it.
4. More and more today there are people who are quite content to sit back and let somebody else go about the business of getting the world's work done while they just idle in comfort in front of their television sets and snicker at the rest of us who must seem pretty stupid to them.
5. We are exhausting our supplies of oil, gas, and coal. Some say this is the cost of progress. Some say we shall find fuel substitutes. Others say that we are on a collision course and that there is nothing we can do about it.

Because modern writers use shorter sentences, it is often thought that their prose lacks style or that if there is style, it is a simple one. People who hold this view are deceived by the prose of earlier writers who seem so obviously to have "style" because their sentence structures were often so elaborate. Although many of them were superb stylists, many of them were also embarrassingly clumsy and imitative. In a way, it is easier to construct an elaborate sentence and give it the stamp of style than it is to write a shorter one and give it true style. If anyone proved this to be true, it was Ernest Hemingway. Long sentences can fool you. They can overpower you with their sheer verbosity. In a long sentence you can get away with things you wouldn't dare in a shorter sentence. You can baffle or bore a reader and make him take the blame for it. A modern writer must be both easy to understand and interesting to read. His sentences must sparkle.

Because modern readers are impatient, they make greater demands on writers than readers ever have before. As a result, we who write cannot slip into the comfortable formulas of the past. Our job is to so develop our writing that it satisfies the demands of the modern reader who, while he values accuracy and speed, still values style.

10. Transition

Although sentences in a paragraph do depend on one another for their structural style, they can still seem isolated and disconnected if they are not linked together by the use of *transition*. Transition is the technique of drawing sentences together, dovetailing them, making them overlap so that the reader's journey from one sentence to the next is not a series of jerks and lunges but a smooth ride on a track he can see ahead of him.

A common way to connect sentences (and paragraphs) is by means of *transitional words* (e.g., however, therefore, moreover, nevertheless, then, consequently) which extend or alter the direction of the sentence that precedes them.

Example
Milly ran out of the house in a panic. *However,* she had enough presence of mind to take her keys with her.

An even more effective way to connect sentences is by repeating key words.

Example
Every winter she made elaborate *plans* to travel the next summer. Every summer her *plans* got curiously mislaid.

Certainly the subtlest and possibly the most effective way to connect sentences is by *repeating key ideas*.

Example
He had not been in the office a week before he sensed a pervasive *climate of suspicion*. It was then that he began to wonder how long he could continue to work comfortably among people who were preoccupied with their *doubts and fears*.

Using Transitional Words

Notice how the transitional words in the following paragraph hold the sentences and the paragraph together.

You really cannot accomplish anything worthwhile if you don't discipline yourself. It is important, *therefore,* to set yourself a schedule and stick to it. Some people believe that they can function on inspiration alone, but after a while they find that the spirit is moving them less and less and they are procrastinating more and more. Without a routine, they have no reason to stay put and keep plodding whether they feel like it or not. *However,* you can also go too far the other way and establish a program that exhausts and discourages you. *Of course,* a little exhaustion and discouragement are a part of anything we do, and they can be healthy antidotes to overconfidence and delusion. *But* they can also be symptoms of an unrealistic approach to a job. The secret is to know your limitations and try not to exceed them beyond a reasonable margin. *Moreover,* it is equally important to know when to break routine, take a day off, work for a while at odd hours, give yourself a little room to breathe. Self-discipline may be the key to achievement, but so is self-preservation. Learn, *then,* to know yourself, and then learn to respect what you know.

You may also have been aware of the repetition of key words or ideas in this paragraph. If so, can you point them out?

Exercise
Add transitional words to this paragraph to connect the sentences smoothly.

Not every woman wants to be liberated. _____,
there are actually some women who prefer the subservient role
of dutiful wife and mother who jumps through her husband's
hoops. _____, such women will throw fits when
they are challenged to be independent. _____, they
constitute a threat to the woman's movement because they are
traitors within the ranks. Women in the movement refuse, _____
_____, to recognize these stubborn defectors as any-
thing short of stupid or deranged. Secretly, however, they hope
to win converts. _____, they continue to proselyt-
ize even while they consider the effort pointless. _____
_____, the non-joiners continue to enjoy the best of both worlds.

Add transitional words to the following sentences.

1. Your body is the only one you have. _____,
   take care of it.
2. It's nice to dream of making it by the time you're thirty. _____
   _____, things don't always work out that way.
3. He's rich enough to buy you out. _____, he's
   likely to make a try.
4. The theatre is usually sold out a week in advance. Try,
   _____, to get your tickets early.
5. This man has been arrested twelve times before. _____
   _____, he has been convicted twice for this very same
   crime.
6. The weather does not look very promising. _____,
   we are going to go ahead with the parade.
7. The blight that attacked the fruit trees early in the summer
   was never treated. _____, the trees died.
8. He's usually very strict about appointments. Under the circumstances, _____, he may agree to see you
   without one.
9. During the tourist season, motels fill up by late afternoon. It
   would be smart, _____, to make reservations
   before you start out.

10. The noise does not seem to be coming from under the hood. The trouble, _____, must be in the exhaust system.

Repeating Key Words

Notice how the repetition of key words in the following paragraph holds the sentences and the paragraph together.

Returning to school in the fall is a ritual that leaves most alumni dewy-eyed with nostalgia. Who can forget the first day *back to school,* the air full of *expectation* and *excitement?* Much of the *excitement* comes from renewing old friendships, and much of the *expectation* lies in wondering what new friends we will make— or what old ones we will lose. But there is also the *excitement* of new *classes* and new *activities.* What will chemistry *class* be like? What will the new typing teacher be like? Will the football team win this year? Will there be time and opportunity for all the *activities* we'd like to engage in? There is also the *excitement* of wearing new clothes and presenting a new image. While we are in school, we change noticeably from one year to the next. We are taller, thinner, prettier—or no taller, no thinner, no prettier, *whatever.* At least we're *different,* or we pray we are. And this year we're going to make that *difference count.* Chances are we're not all that *different,* and if we are, we don't make it *count* all that much; but *whatever* happens to us, we can never forget the hope that stirred us in September, and we tend to go on through life with spirits highest as the calendar year winds down but the school year is just beginning to get wound up.

Exercise
Fill in the blanks in the following paragraph with key words from previous sentences.

Some people manipulate others by outbursts of emotion. They know the power of tears, anger, enthusiasm and use these _____ _____ to influence the susceptible. Some wives, for example, know how to use _____ to get their way; and some children _____ throw a tantrum and get

results. Not all _____ are in-
sincere, of course, but when the person experiencing the _____
_____ has more to gain than just the release of tension,
there is good reason to be skeptical. The sincere _____
is one that calls for nothing more than a polite response from us.
We commiserate with someone's sorrow, or we delight in someone's joy. When, however, we are expected to alleviate that _____
_____ or preserve that _____ —when, in
short, we are made to feel responsible for the other person's
mood—then we can begin to question the sincerity of the _____
_____. A person who lets us know that his happiness
depends on what we do to maintain it is trying to make us feel
guilty. If, indeed, we give in and do feel _____,
then we are being manipulated. When that happens, then that
and only that is what we should feel _____ about.

After each sentence in the following list, write a sentence in
which you repeat a key word but still carry the idea forward.

1. Drinking has become a major problem among teenagers. _____
   _____

2. They presented the play to an audience they thought would
   hate it. _____
   _____

3. The suspect had an airtight alibi. _____
   _____

4. Cheating has become a major headache for college instructors. _____
   _____

5. She loved loud music, and she listened to it day and night.
   _____

6. It's almost impossible to hang a picture and keep it straight.
   _____
   _____

7. Good posture is something you have to work at. _____
   _____

8. As coffee prices soar, more people are drinking tea. _____
_____

9. Many people would love to throw a great party, but they really
   don't know how to go about it. _____
_____

10. The path to fame is often strewn with heartaches. _____
_____

Repeating Key Ideas

Notice how the repetition of key ideas in the following paragraph
holds the sentences and the paragraph together.

It is easy to be deluded into believing that you really want
something when, in reality, you don't really want it at all. You
pursue a dream, and if you are unlucky enough to have that dream
come true, it *turns out to be a nightmare.* Let's say, for instance,
that you think you want to act, not because you really have any
talent but because you have fallen in love with the idea of acting
or with a particular stage or screen idol. You aren't content to
live the life of a *star* vicariously, fantasizing the fame you have
no business pursuing. No, you have to enroll in drama school
and make yourself the target of scorn and ridicule. You can take
it, though, because you know that *hatred* is a sign of envy, and
it's all part of paying your dues. You won't give up. You don't
give up. Somehow, by sheer *perseverance,* you fall into a part that
does make you famous, and soon you are falling apart. Your privacy is gone, your values are confused, your friends become
enemies, your enemies try to become your friends. You discover
that you're not a swinger, that you are basically simple at heart,
that you crave anonymity. You hate the cheap thrills and the tacky
glamour. You just long to sit again in the balcony and let the
shadows float before your glazed eyes. Only this time while you
sit there, you won't kid yourself. The pity is that by then it's too
late.

You can see that (a) "pursue a dream" echoes "you really want
something"; (b) "turns out to be a nightmare" echoes "you don't

really want it at all"; (c) "star" echoes "stage or screen idol"; (d) "hatred" echoes "scorn and ridicule"; (e) "perseverance" echoes "won't give up," "don't give up"; and (f) after "falling apart" the rest of the paragraph specifies "how"; the transition is effected by means of analysis.

Exercise

Identify the repetition of key ideas in the following paragraph and explain how it works to effect transition from one sentence to another and to hold the paragraph together.

Limited opportunity can be a great incentive. If there are no restrictions on what you can do, you may have trouble making up your mind. Should you make a wrong decision, you'll wish you had chosen one of the many other possibilities. When opportunity is limited, your freedom of choice is likewise limited, and chances are you will exercise that freedom more cautiously. Rather than making a random choice, one that may have more glitter than gold to it, you will choose more realistically, perhaps even with the feeling that you are being forced to settle for less than you wanted. This compromise can motivate you to make the best of what you have. It can spark your determination to outdo yourself. It can inspire you to greater heights than you ever would have reached had you had your way. Knowing that it may be your only chance, you fight to win. And maybe down deep you are blessed with the happy suspicion that this struggle is, after all, a dance with destiny.

Go back through this paragraph and check for the other two kinds of transitional techniques, particularly the repetition of key words.

Exercise

After each sentence in the following list add a second sentence that demonstrates transition by the technique of repeating key ideas.

1. The devil finds work for idle hands. _____

_____

2. With two eyes and one tongue, we should see more than we
   say. _____
   _____

3. A person feels he has won an argument if he has the last
   word. _____
   _____

4. In bad weather you need transportation that is dependable.
   _____

5. Fretful is the man with insatiable desires. _____
   _____

6. Some ex-convicts live in rooms that resemble cells. _____
   _____

7. Misfortune tends to strike when we least expect it. _____
   _____

8. In modern life, privacy is a luxury. _____
   _____

9. A bigot is a person who will defend to the death your right
   to agree with him. _____
   _____

10. It's possible to disagree without being disagreeable. _____
    _____

A word of caution: try not to let your transition seem too obvious
or deliberate. Examples and exercises will always show their
seams because they are contrived to emphasize a single point or
technique. In your ordinary writing, you want to be conscious of
the need for transition, but you want to be equally conscious of
the need to tuck it in so that the reader senses it but is not distracted by it.

11. Paragraphs

A paragraph consists of several interrelated sentences that develop a single topic in a consistent tone and style. Although a paragraph is usually one segment of a whole essay, it should, with few exceptions, be complete enough in itself to be meaningful in isolation. While our interest in this chapter is primarily in the way paragraphs can be given style, we will necessarily be concerned also with the other characteristics that contribute to the making of a well-written paragraph.

A fully developed paragraph includes the following:

1. an indication of the topic clear enough to be identified, usually stated in a sentence (or two) at or near the beginning of the paragraph, but appearing elsewhere as circumstances dictate
2. a sufficient number of supporting sentences to allow reasonably thorough development of the topic
3. a discernible relationship between each supporting sentence and the declared topic
4. effective transition between sentences
5. a conclusive ending
6. consistent and appropriate tone

7. consistent and appropriate style
8. consistent and appropriate content

Here is the rough draft of a paragraph that violates many of these principles. The analysis that follows will clarify what these principles mean.

Outer Space

I'm more impressed by a symphony than a galaxy. I know my mind is supposed to boggle over the immeasurable vastness of outer space and the innumerable suns and planets, exploding, dying, rotating, revolving, disappearing into unfathomable black holes; but when I behold the night's starred face, it is not into nothingness I sink but into a stupor. My neck aches, my eyes water, and I always end up in an argument over which dipper is which. I guess what I'm thinking is, sure, it's staggering and all that—all those countless pinpricks out there that are really a lot bigger than we think and probably hotter than blazes—but what can I do about it except exclaim, "How fantastic! How incredible!" and then go on about my business. What really astounds me about what's out there is not what's out there so much as my mind's ability to be astounded. The stars cannot be astounded; I can. They are products of creation; I am both product and participant. They have no power over themselves; I have the power to create new things. The spark of divine fire that produces a symphony is more precious to me than a billion galaxies expanding and contracting in endless space because that spark transcends mere matter and allies me with the power that set the heavens in motion.

Analysis

1. The topic sentence could be either the first one or the fifth one. It's not clear because the paragraph goes in two directions. When the paragraph is revised, a new topic sentence should be written.
2. There seem to be enough sentences to do the job, but since the topic is unclear, it's hard to tell. As a flat statement of a

very personal point of view, the paragraph could not really stand more than six or eight sentences of development.

3. Here's where the trouble begins. If the first sentence is the topic sentence, then the "symphony" idea is neglected until the end, where it is only confusing. If the fifth sentence is the topic sentence, then little that precedes it really anticipates it, and what follows is only obliquely related to it.

4. Transition suffers by the third or fourth sentence when the direction of the paragraph shifts.

5. The concluding sentence sounds like a grand finale all right, but it is out of line with most of what precedes it.

6. The real problem begins to surface here. The light, mocking tone of the first half of the paragraph is inconsistent with the solemn, even pompous tone of the last half. The author can't make up his mind whether he wants to be funny or serious.

7. The shift in style, of course, contributes to the shift in tone— and in content. At first the style is breezy and irreverent; the language is informal, and there is parody and humor. Later the language becomes formal, the sentences balanced, the imagery exalted.

8. The content is confused. Is the author ridiculing the astronomy freaks? Is he merely confessing his own lack of interest? Is he praising the mind's capacity for awe and wonder? Is he praising man's creative powers? Or is he praising God? You cannot say in one breath that space bores you and in the next that you are astounded by it.

Revision I

In this revision the humor is emphasized and the solemnity omitted.

The Empire Strikes Out

I'm not impressed by outer space. I know my mind is supposed to boggle over its inconceivable vastness, its innumerable galaxies, its immeasurable suns and moons, planets and stars, comets

and meteors, shrinking, expanding, exploding, burning, disappearing into the maws of monstrous black holes. But it all leaves
me cold. When I behold the night's starred face, it is not into
nothingness I sink but into a stupor. My neck aches, my eyes
water, and I never know which dipper is which. Even the doom-
mongers don't scare me. What am I supposed to do when they
tell me that in a billion years or so the earth will freeze over or
melt or collide with the sun or vanish in a star war? What do I
do when they tell me that poor little Earth is an insignificant
planet in an insignificant galaxy hurtling helplessly doomward at
a zillion light years per something or other? Only an ego like Carl
Sagan's could find that exciting. I can't even get up the enthusiasm to find it depressing. I just want things the way they were:
a shine on that harvest moon, a twinkle in that little star. Oh,
how I wish the earth were flat again.

Exercise
1. Compare this revision with the original and then analyze it
   according to the principles of good paragraphing.
2. Analyze the word choice in sentences 8, 10, and 11. How does
   it contribute to the effect?
3. Identify two or three examples of complex sentence structure
   and explain their style and appropriateness.
4. So much is packed into that one little word that ends the essay
   (*again*). What does it do and say?

Revision II

In this revision the humor is subdued and the seriousness emphasized.

Mind and Matter
I find it patronizing the way the popularizers of astronomy flaunt
their obsession with outer space before me as if they created it
and I'm too dumb to grasp it. If I act unimpressed, they browbeat
me with incomprehensible statistics calculated to frighten me into
submission. What they fail to see is that I am as impressed as

they are, but what impresses me about outer space is less its existence than the fact that I have a mind capable of being impressed by it. Instead of feeling insignificant when confronted with the size and age of the universe, I rejoice in the knowledge that I have been endowed with the ability not only to comprehend but to create; and this knowledge makes me proud. If I did not have this ability, I would not even know how to feel insignificant. What has already been created is wonderful indeed, but the fact that my mind can carry creation forward is, to me, even more wonderful. Whereas these space enthusiasts would like me to be astounded by what's going on out there, I am astounded by the power within me to add to what's going on here—*and* there. The triumph of creation is a mind capable of appreciating that creation and of contributing to it.

Exercise

1. Which is the topic sentence?
2. In a paragraph of opinion, many of the sentences will be restatements of that opinion rather than hard facts. Where does such restatement occur in this paragraph?
3. Check each sentence to see if it supports the topic.
4. Circle the transitional words and phrases that connect one sentence to another.
5. Although "I" is used, how personal is this paragraph? Is the use of the first person justified: How does it affect the tone, the style, and the content?
6. What's wrong with the following as the final sentence: "Creation's greatest creation is a creature who can create"? This is, after all, what the author means, isn't it?
7. The word "impress" is used three times in one sentence. Is such repetition justifiable?

On the left is a rough draft and on the right a revision of a paragraph on paranoids. Compare them according to the check list of the principles of paragraphing listed at the beginning of the chapter, paying close attention to the differences in style.

Portrait of a Paranoid

A paranoid is a person who thinks everybody is out to get him, and he's not always wrong. He knows that when the phone rings, it's either a death or a crank, that his neighbors are spying on him, and that the police are going to knock on his door at four in the morning and drag him away. He knows that when he enters a room, everybody drops everything to stare at him. He knows people laugh behind his back and lie to his face. He expects the alarm to go off when he goes through an airport security check. He expects to have his luggage opened at customs and his house ransacked while he is gone. Each payday he looks for a pink slip in his envelope. When the mail comes, he looks for a subpoena, an IRS audit, or a letter bomb. Everywhere he looks he sees conspiracy, and he is the target. He expects to be blackmailed, framed, brainwashed, and eventually exiled. Sooner or later he knows somebody's going to blow the whistle, push the button, pull the plug, call in the chips, stop the music, halt the train, jump the gun, put out a contract, turn the screw, spring the trap. No wonder even paranoids have enemies!

Praise be to paranoids. Nothing surprises them. They're sure that their phone is bugged, that the neighbors are spying on them, and that the goons are going to hammer on their door in the middle of the night and take them hostage. People stare when they enter a room, laugh behind their backs, and lie to their faces. When they travel, they get frisked at the airport and grilled by customs, and while they're gone, their house is being ransacked and their car hot wired. They look for pink slips in their paychecks, subpoenas in their mail, and bombs under their hood. They see conspiracy everywhere, and they are the target. Every friend is an informant and every stranger a hit man. Any day they expect to be blackmailed, framed, brainwashed, arrested, tortured, and executed. Sooner or later they know somebody's going to blow the whistle, push the button, pull the switch, jump the gun, turn the screw, spring the trap, lower the boom. No wonder even paranoids have enemies!

Analysis of the Revision

The topic sentence is stated at the beginning of the paragraph and is developed by means of a series of examples of paranoia with references along the way to the paranoid's lack of surprise: "They're sure that," "They look for," "they expect," "they know." The examples are of common fears, exaggerated by their sheer number.

Word choice tends to be slangy in keeping with the satirical tone of the paragraph. Words like "bugged," "goons," "frisked," "hot wired," along with the clichés that conclude the paragraph, are the jargon of paranoia. Wordiness is avoided by compressing many of the fears into a series within a sentence and eliminating introductory words like "They are just waiting for" from many of the sentences. The reader knows that when he reads, "People stare when they enter a room," this is in the mind of the paranoid. The context makes the imaginary fears implicit.

Transition is effected mostly by the repetition of the pronoun referring to paranoids. The shift to the plural pronoun in the revision is in keeping with the opening two sentences, which would be ruined if they were made singular. The plural also universalizes the experience; the singular finally gives the impression that there is only one such creature loose. Transitional words are unnecessary because of the repetition of the pronoun as well as the similarity between the examples. No sentences digress from the topic, and there is a sufficient number of them to develop the topic. Their number and length in the rough draft reduce the impact of the paragraph.

The tone is uniformly light and mocking, the style lean and loose, and the content graphic and consistent.

Exercise

Write and revise a paragraph (about one of these: hypochondriacs, skeptics, pushovers, cowards) in which you begin with the topic sentence and then develop it by means of examples. Model it as closely as you can on the structure and spirit of the sample paragraph.

On the left is a rough draft and on the right a revision of a paragraph on college athletes. Compare the two, mainly for stylistic differences, and then check them against the list of the principles of paragraph writing.

The Professional Amateur

In the old days a college football player was a guy who went to college and just happened to play football. Today he is a guy who plays football and just happens to go to college. Gone is the day of the happy coincidence that saw a coach's dream quarterback innocently matriculating at the college of his choice. These days that quarterback's choice is the college that makes him the best offer. Gone also is the occasional scrimmage sandwiched in between French class and chemistry lab or even sacrificed for the sake of a term paper. Today's college athlete hardly needs to know how to speak English, and his locker room is the only lab he needs. He may never make it to the library, but it doesn't matter if he can make it to the Dust Bowl. He is a subsidized robot programmed to get out there on the astroturf and bring tears to the bloodshot eyes of aging alumni. He learns that playing ball is hard work, and even

There was a time when a college football player was a guy who went to college and just happened to play football. Today he is a guy who plays football and just happens to go to college. Gone is the day when a coach stood biting his fingernails at registration, hoping to spot a promising quarterback among the incoming freshmen. These days that quarterback has been recruited, and the "college of his choice" is the one that offers him the best deal. Gone also is the day of the occasional scrimmage sandwiched in between English class and chemistry lab or even sacrificed for the sake of a term paper. Today's college athlete hasn't much use for English, and his locker room is all the lab he knows. If he wants to make it to graduation, he doesn't make it to the library first; he makes it to the Dust Bowl. He is a mercenary paid to get out there on the astroturf and bring tears to the bloodshot eyes of aging alumni. He

though he's playing at the am- | may be playing amateur ball,
ateur level, he's no amateur. but he is no amateur. He's a
He's a professional. And that's professional. And that's what's
what's so depressing about it. so depressing about it all, the
Amateur sports are no longer fact that amateur sports are no
for amateurs. longer for amateurs.

Analysis Exercise
1. Which is the topic sentence?
2. Explain the connotations of the following words and expressions:
   just happened (sentence 1)
   biting his fingernails (sentence 2)
   makes him an offer versus offers him a deal (sentence 4)
   hasn't much use for English (sentence 6)
   all the lab he needs versus all the lab he knows (sentence 6)
   make it (sentence 7)
   mercenary (sentence 8)
   bloodshot eyes (sentence 8)
3. What kind of a sentence is sentence 1?
4. Analyze sentence 7.
5. The conclusion of the rough draft is grammatically correct; the
   conclusion of the revision is idiomatic. How would you defend the revision over the original?
6. What does "Dust Bowl" tell you about the tone of this paragraph?
7. Can you speak to the accuracy of the content?

Writing Exercise
Write a paragraph (about one of these: professional students;
weekend warriors; coaches; gourmet cooks; fortune tellers; self-
styled experts) in which you withhold stating the topic sentence
until the end. Use the sample paragraph as a model.

Here for your analysis is the final draft of a paragraph on airing
your emotions.

Letting Off Steam

In the old days they used to talk about "venting your spleen" because they thought that the spleen, believed to be the organ of ill temper, would rupture if it were not periodically bled. It's an interesting notion. Anyone who has experienced the catharsis of a rip-roaring temper tantrum knows the exhilaration that comes from opening up all the valves. You might call it emotional jogging, for when you lose your temper, you exercise emotional muscles otherwise in danger of atrophy. Within us are strong feelings that need to be released now and then in order to cleanse the mind. Although you can overdo it, an occasional outburst can be downright therapeutic. In short, letting off steam is good for you. If nothing else, it keeps the old juices flowing. If you don't fly off the handle now and then, you'll turn into an emotional zombie with no feeling for anything.

Analysis

1. Which is the topic sentence?
2. What synonyms are used for "letting off steam"?
3. What synonyms are used for "venting"?
4. How would you characterize the tone? (serious? smug? halfhearted? scathing? mocking? indignant? apologetic? pious? ironic?)

Writing Exercise
Write a paragraph in which you defend some form of behavior usually considered improper. (Possibilities: swearing, scolding, writing graffiti, making crude gestures, belching, heckling, crowding ahead, double parking, jaywalking, label switching)

This last paragraph is a definition of "apology." Analyze it according to the list of the principles of paragraph writing. Try to judge the accuracy and honesty of the content.

Excuse for an Apology

An apology is not a confession of guilt but a request for reinstatement into someone's good graces. We say "I'm sorry" as often as we say "How are you," and both are expressions of good will, not of bad conscience. When we apologize, what we are asking the other person to do is not to excuse us but to accept us; for basically we really don't think we have done anything we need to be excused for, but we do have a need for acceptance. In other words, when we ask someone to "accept" our apologies, we are silently asking him to take us back and not hold a grudge. What we are sorry for is that we have risked rejection, not that we have truly behaved unjustly. An apology is a balancing act between integrity and popularity. If we offend someone, we can rationalize it easily enough. What bothers us later is not what we did but that the other person didn't take it right. The way we clear this up is to call it a "misunderstanding." That way we can have our say and still keep our friend. The simple truth is that people can live neither with guilt nor without friends; hence the invention of the apology, the truce between ethics and etiquette.

Analysis

1. Point out an example of a balanced sentence. There are several.
2. Identify incidences of "antithesis."
3. What kind of a sentence is sentence 3?
4. Explain the construction of the concluding sentence.

Writing Exercise

Write a paragraph in which you attempt a rather unorthodox definition of a common social interchange. Some possibilities are: condolences (glad it's not me); congratulations (wish it were me); commiseration (glad it's you); asking a favor (using someone?); doing a favor (interfering?).

The emphasis in this chapter has been on the organization, development, and overall style of the paragraph and not on its function within the context of the whole essay. Opening, closing, and transitional paragraphs, while they differ in function from paragraphs of topic development, still abide by the principles relating to tone, style, and content. They are to the whole essay what opening, closing, and transitional sentences are to the paragraph; for a paragraph is, after all, a microcosm of an essay. In the sections that follow, you will be writing both paragraphs and full essays. Remember as you do that the principles for writing either are essentially the same, and the key to both is consistency.

IV

Manipulations

Part of knowing how to use style is knowing how to abuse it.
Poets know this. They have their doggerel days when they get
the puns and bad rhymes and sticky sentiment out of their systems. Artists know this. Every painter has his waterfalls and sun-
sets and storms at sea stashed away in a closet somewhere. Composers know this. For every great song they write there's a stack
of tacky tunes tucked away in some piano bench.

The very essence of creativity is freedom, and for you as a writer
this means the freedom to experiment with all styles of writing,
good and bad, without risk, as you develop a style of your own.
Bad style, incidentally, does not mean bad grammar. You won't
be asked, as you go through the exercises in this section, to be
sloppy about spelling or punctuation or noun-verb agreement.
What you will be asked to do is to analyze and then practice the
techniques whereby writers, either by accident or design, use
style in wicked or woolly ways.

Style is abused when, either intentionally or unintentionally, it is obscure, misleading, evasive, imitative, or just plain "cute." It is abused when it separates the reader from the content by dragging in a red herring, throwing up a smoke screen, confusing him, alienating him, or insulting his intelligence. When your style smothers your content, you are not playing fair with your readers. It's one thing to guide them, to arouse or amuse them, as you inform them; it's something else to toy with them, to be devious and cunning, to manipulate them in a patronizing manner. Writers who do this generally write propaganda, but they can also be found writing campaign speeches, replies to customer complaints, advertising copy, and feature stories for tabloids.

Most of us abuse style accidentally. We don't mean to do it; we just fall into it, and more than likely don't know how we got there or how we can get out. The purpose of this section is to help you find out how you got there and how you can get out. Fortunately, the experience is not an unpleasant one. Bad style can be as enjoyable as a bad habit.

In the opening chapter on the *obscure style,* you will be writing the sort of foggy prose you find too often in instruction manuals and test booklets. Obscurity is a virtue only if your phone is being tapped or your mail censored; it is a discourtesy if you have information other people need or want but can't make sense out of when you impart it. Once you see how innocently it happens, you will be better prepared to be on your guard against it. If you persist in being obscure, then the only hope for you is either poetry or politics.

The next style you will learn to write and then reject is the *misleading style.* Although you may never be guilty of deliberately suppressing information, you may inadvertently omit relevant information or give what you say a slant you didn't intend. You can also be misleading by drawing faulty conclusions, confusing two issues, or making illogical connections—or through vagueness or exaggeration. In a sense, all bad style is misleading because its purpose or its effect is to lead readers astray, to muddle their perceptions and corrupt their judgment.

A style common to people in an awkward situation is the *diversionary style*. They lapse into it when the subject is too touchy and they would really rather talk about something else. What they do is work the subject around to one they feel more comfortable with and thereby divert your attention from the main issue. Politicians do this when they take a question and tailor their response to fit a ready-made answer. Writers do this when they let themselves get sidetracked until they are completely off the subject.

Another popular abuse of style is the use of the *imitative style*. The imitative style is formula writing, writing that conforms mindlessly to the worn-out traditions of a particular group. It can be found in business letters, interoffice memos, lab reports, government documents, small-town newspapers, textbooks, and, alas, august professional journals. Wherever it's found, it should be stamped out.

Last—and maybe least—we come to the most seductive stylistic abuse of all, the *confessional style*, a style all too dear to the hearts of aspiring writers and one whose budding should be nipped. It's an autobiographical style that cloys quickly. It's the style that tells the world that you are worth reading about, that what you have seen and done, thought and felt are important enough for someone else to waste his time on. Confessions almost invariably sound boastful and self-serving; and although there are a few classic ones around, most of the time this sort of writing is merely embarrassing. It's a style best left to convicts, converts, and call girls whose phones have stopped ringing. If it just weren't so darned irresistible!

This section provides you with a rare opportunity to nibble at forbidden fruit and get away with it. As long as you don't acquire a taste for it, you should find the experience nourishing as well as refreshing.

Have fun!

12 . The Obscure Style

You might think that instruction in obfuscation is about as necessary as instruction in how to fudge on your income tax. Everybody does it, so who needs to be taught how? The trouble is that this most common of all writing ailments has thus far failed to respond to either shock treatment or massive doses of blue pencil or red ink. The admonition, "Be clear!" is about as helpful as "Have a nice day." It's a nice idea, but how do you go about doing it? The way we're going to go about doing it in this chapter is to find out what happens when our writing becomes obscure, analyze what we learn, and then write some deliberately muddled prose.

The two pillars of obscurity are ignorance and confusion. The writer either doesn't know what he's talking about or gets rattled when he does. There are, however, some writers who are neither ignorant nor confused but who write as if they were in order to purposely puzzle the reader. Since they know the rules you are about to learn and deliberately write the way you are going to write (in this chapter), let's take a look at what they do.

Example 1
Imagine that a corporate executive is worried about fluctuations in the oil market and what they will mean to a delicately bal-

anced international market. He needs time to study the situation carefully before he issues any statements because he knows that whatever he says will have immediate effects on the stock market, on related companies, and, of course, on his own company and himself. He decides to call a meeting, but he does not want the members who will attend to be able to leak any information or even to become anxious. Therefore, he sends them the following memo:

The purpose of the meeting shall be, should the question arise, or should you be uncertain about it yourselves, to reassess those priorities directly affecting the realignment of assignments, contingent upon the fluctuations within the market complex as they are presently manifesting themselves in the context of a global effort to readjust existing fiscal commitments. Prior to the present time there has been little or no opportunity to examine policies and procedures impinging upon the problem area as it has been defined in view of recent developments concerning unanticipated alterations in matters related to the principal participants and their constituents, a deficiency which could impose severe restrictions and result in serious ramifications within the structure as it presently exists at this particular point in time.

Exercise
Identify and discuss the following techniques of obfuscation that are used in this paragraph:

1. complex sentence structure
2. inflated diction
3. density (compacted language)
4. redundancy

Example 2
In the following paragraph, the author, as Oscar Wilde once put it, "has nothing to say, and says it." The chief gimmick here is repetition. The first sentence, whatever it means, is merely restated throughout the paragraph.

His greatest fault was also his greatest asset: reason. It was for him a double-edged sword that cut both ways, moving as it did, in one direction at one time, and in the opposite direction at another. When he wanted to, he could use reason to good advantage; but there were other times when, deliberately nor not—and no one can be sure—his use of the faculty of reason was positively inimical to his professed interests and concerns. Apparently, he either never did understand the paradoxical power of reason and, therefore, failed to be in control of it; or, as some think, he understood it only too well and chose either not to control it or to ignore it altogether. Nevertheless, it was reason that brought him to the top in the beginning, and it was also reason that brought him down in the end.

Exercise

Can you find redundancy in this paragraph? complex sentence structure? anything else? Develop one of the following non-ideas in one obscure paragraph, using whatever techniques work.

1. Her beauty was her salvation and her downfall.
2. Some men have worked for more and received less.
3. The times are neither better nor worse than they are.

Example 3

A common way to be obscure is to give with one hand and take away with the other. The way to do this is to begin on what sounds like a solid, positive note and then qualify your position until finally you have undermined it entirely, leaving the reader he knows not where.

I suppose you could call it a successful film. I don't mean successful in the financial sense or, for that matter, in the artistic sense either. Certainly it was not popular at the box office, and critics were generally unresponsive. When I speak of success, I am thinking of something else entirely. To me a film is successful if it breaks new ground, introduces new talent, experiments with new techniques. Although this film breaks no really new ground, it does take a novel approach to some familiar territory. As for

new talent, if none of it is especially promising, at least it is unfamiliar. Whether the techniques are new or accidental is, after
all, irrelevant. What does it really matter, unless one worries that
what is accidental cannot be repeated. But then, the best art is
inimitable, and although this film is not exactly art—good, better, or best—it is inimitable; and that counts for something. Perhaps what I'm saying is that total failure is, in a way, a kind of
success, isn't it?

Exercise

After you have analyzed the way in which the author of this
paragraph undermines his own stand, try doing the same thing
with one of the following statements.

1. This book belongs on the bestseller list.
2. She is just possibly one of the most gifted artists around.
3. Certainly he deserves more recognition than he has been given.

Example 4

Literary analysis is such an easy target, it seems cheap to take a
shot at it. Perhaps obscurity is common there because so much
has been written about so little that only the obscure is left to
deal with, and the way to deal with it is to make sure that it
remains obscure. (How's that for making the obscure obscure?)
In the following paragraph, all the writer wanted to say was that
nothing lasts, neither love nor roses; but he knows how far that
will get him, so he opts for obfuscation. Examine the diction
carefully. Check also for redundancy.

"O My Luve's like a red, red rose, / That's newly sprung in
June" can best be seen in the light of archetypal totemic polari-
zation. "Luve," [sic] an abstraction, is counterpoised with "rose,"
a concretion, and both are transfixed within the context of the
pivotal month of June, part spring, part summer. Archetypically,
love, "which endureth," is compared with the mortal rose in a
transient season, suggesting that love, too, is mortal and will
surely die. The mind, inclined to seek absolutes, yet compelled
to accept relatives, must believe simultaneously in the illusion of

permanence and the reality of mutability. The repetition of the sanguinarily suggestive "red, red" reinforces the illusion of permanence while the phrase "newly sprung," having as it does no opposite ("oldly sprung"?), reminds us that mutability is constantly changing (springing) and that by the end of June, spring will already have "sprung."

Exercise

Check the fourth sentence for awkward word choice and arrangement. Aside from being obscure, what else is wrong with this paragraph? Choose one of the following familiar lines of poetry and say something simple about it in a long and obscure paragraph.

1. "This is the forest primeval, the murmuring pines and the hemlocks"
2. "O rose, thou art sick!"
3. "How changed is here each spot man makes or fills!"

Example 5

Storytellers sometimes owe their success to a quality of obscurity which they have down pat and which their readers come to expect. Perhaps, when this brand of obfuscation is in the field, it means that readers are more interested in impressions than in meanings. The trouble with this theory is that it doesn't seem to work with the more respected but decidedly less popular purveyors of the obscure: James (in the later novels), Joyce (everywhere but in *Dubliners*, and even there at times), Proust, Woolf, Barth, Pynchon. The difference is probably this: while the celebrated authors painstakingly encode their writing to deliver meaning to those willing to decode it, the pulp writers just prattle along, never quite sure where they're going, but sounding, to the lazy ear, as if they are. Read the following paragraph through quickly to see what meaning you pick up. Chances are you'll come away with something, although it's likely that each reader could come away with something else. Then go back and try to figure out just how the subjects and objects and modifiers and phrases are supposed to match up.

They were happy to move to the new house in Kent which was not far from where they had lived before, coming as they were from less spacious surroundings, unfortunately part and parcel of the life they were forced to live amidst, as it were, the alien corn. Deborah, dear child, happiest with her doll, whose heart was never good, pined away giddily at its loss, vowing never again to form an attachment which was an unhappy thing because of an aching need inside her to love and be loved in return for which she would have given her murmuring heart, as if it were really hers, as she knew, to give away, when deep inside it she knew it had been taken—nay, stolen!—by one not so inanimate, yet not, alas, animated sufficiently to please her. To whom, pray tell, was she to turn, or return, as it were, if it were not to those who were, if what were said were true, the very ones who were to be her guardians, were they willing, as she was, were it only for a little while, especially if things were to be the way they were?

Exercise

Can you find any actual mistakes in grammar or syntax? Study the "were's" in the last sentence and see if anything can be done about them. Try writing a similar paragraph in which you get your modifiers scrambled and in which you also let a word or a turn of phrase or a particular structure carry you away. Be sure to pile phrase upon phrase and clause upon clause.

Can you find a paragraph in anything you have read recently (student newspaper, textbook) that qualifies for inclusion in this chapter? Can you find a paragraph elsewhere in this book that qualifies for inclusion in this chapter?

Not all writing that seems obscure is obscure. Much depends on the reader's intelligence and particularly his prior knowledge of and interest in the matter at hand. Writing geared to specific professions (e.g., medicine, law, physics) would be obscure to most people but clear to those in the field, provided, of course, that the writing conforms to the accepted standards of that field. It must be said, however, that there are writers publishing in professional journals who too often purvey a brand of intentional obfuscation which is calculated to exclude outsiders. It takes courage to resist this kind of institutionalized obscurity, but resist it we must. No self-respecting writer who wishes to develop an original style can afford not to.

What we have been dealing with in this chapter is inexcusable obscurity, largely unintentional, in the sort of prose supposedly intended to be read by the average person of reasonable intelligence. Now that you have learned the ogre's tricks, it is to be hoped that you will never again, either wittingly or unwittingly, wander into his lair.

13. The Misleading Style

The misleading style is, essentially, the style of propaganda, which is the handmaiden of prejudice and deceit. It is never harmless, but it can be innocent; and although innocence is often a more fearful adversary than intent, it can, at least, be forgiven. We all mislead unintentionally—out of ignorance, out of fear, out of misguided tact. Maybe we don't know all the facts, maybe we are afraid to be frank, maybe we think we are being kind. Whatever the reason, it is probably easier to be misleading, accidentally, than it is to be fair.

The purpose of propaganda is to mislead intentionally. It is an "art" that has been refined in this century and put to all sorts of nefarious uses. The senates and cemeteries of the world are filled with the misleaders and the misled. Hitler knew the power of propaganda well and even appointed Goebbels to head a Propaganda Ministry. Hitler himself, however, was a past master at the art, and it is interesting to note that when he was frank in *Mein Kampf*, few paid any attention, but when he was devious, as in the famous "Peace Speech" of May 17, 1933, everyone listened and was taken in. The speech was given in reply to President Roosevelt's worldwide disarmament proposal. It unified the German people and impressed the outside world. Here is an excerpt:

The proposal made by President Roosevelt, of which I learned last night, has earned the warmest thanks of the German government. It is prepared to agree to this method of overcoming the international crisis. . . . The President's proposal is a ray of comfort for all who wish to co-operate in the maintenance of peace. . . . Germany is entirely ready to renounce all offensive weapons if the armed nations, on their side, will destroy their offensive weapons. . . . Germany would also be perfectly ready to disband her entire military establishment and destroy the small amount of arms remaining to her, if the neighboring countries will do the same. . . . Germany is prepared to agree to any solemn pact of nonaggression, because she does not think of attacking but only of acquiring security.

Elsewhere in the speech Hitler called war "unlimited madness" that would "cause the collapse of the present social and political order." Because a statement like this made it "sound" as if he was against war, people were ready to believe that he really was. What they failed to listen for was the "catch": equality of treatment. When, later, the Allies balked on this one, Hitler had the excuse he was looking for to invalidate the bargain.

As we have seen before, willingness to believe is often a writer's (or speaker's) greatest asset. This leads to the most infamous variation on the misleading style: the Big Lie. Hitler's technique was to put the blame for the lie on those who could not accept a condition which he adroitly tucked into the seams of the lie.

At the risk of "putting a gun into the hands of a baby," we are going to analyze and imitate the misleading style in this chapter more as a means of coping with it than of copying it. Forewarned is forearmed. It is a devilishly tempting style to use in a pinch, but the gun can backfire. Knowledge of it will do you better service as a means of detecting propaganda when it is in the field. As usual, the best way to know how something is done is to do it yourself.

Here are some of the unwholesome techniques of the misleading style:

1. shift emphasis: distort; accentuate the trivial, minimize the significant; rearrange priorities
2. omit things: like qualifications, distractions, contradictions
3. introduce irrelevancies: sidetrack; digress
4. distort diction: use either flat or inflated language, depending on what you want to play down or play up
5. draw questionable comparisons: use shaky analogies ("dissenters are thorns among the roses")
6. use innuendo: imply evil consequences; inpute ulterior motives; suggest suspicions
7. ask leading or rhetorical questions
8. beg the question ("We must be strong, for strength is peace.")
9. pander to prejudices: appeal to bigotry and ignorance
10. sound authoritative: come from the mountaintop

Example 1

An editorial writer is constant prey to the temptation to mislead. In his eagerness to promote his opinion, he cannot help giving a slant to the information underlying his editorial. Analyze the following editorial according to the techniques of the misleading style.

No sooner had the basketball season ended than, without any warning whatsoever, Coach Johnson was called in by the Athletic Director and summarily fired. The Athletic Council, which reviews such matters, had met briefly just prior to the firing and agreed unanimously to support the director's decision. Although the firing came as a surprise to Johnson, it is a well-known fact that the Athletic Director has long had it in for Johnson and has been out to get him for some time. It is also common knowledge that the council has always rubber-stamped anything the director wants.

The members of the council—seven white males and two token white females (who know nothing about basketball)—refused to comment on the firing except to say that it was done according to prescribed procedure. What sort of a procedure is it that allows a man to be thrown out of a job this late in the year and without the least notification? If he could not have been forewarned, could not Coach Johnson have been counselled during the season and at least given a fighting chance to prove himself? Under pressure to win, win, win, is he not a victim of the very society which has pledged minorities a head start? The director claims that the team did not play well enough. We think he means that the team did not *win* often enough. The director says Johnson is being let go because he is not a good coach. We think he is being let go because he is not a *white* coach.

Johnson filed suit on the basis of discrimination but later withdrew when the university agreed to settle out of court and award Johnson damages. Isn't this "pay-off" admission of guilt? When are we going to shape up and stop giving blacks the choice between the auction block and the chopping block?

Exercise
Can you figure out the true story from the account just given? Try to write an editorial in which you defend the dismissal of the coach in an equally misleading manner.

Example 2
Travel literature is notoriously slanted. Ordinary people who have gone someplace and had a miserable time would rather die than say their time and money were wasted. If they can drag out the slides and tell you what a wonderful time they had, think of the travel writers who get paid to sell you the same package. Here is a misleading promotional *Spiel* from East Germany, where propaganda is alive and well and flourishing in Leipzig.

Leipzig may not be Paris, but it is fast becoming the fun city of Eastern Europe. In August, when the historic annual trade fair takes place, visitors from around the world can see displays from some of the world's leading manufacturers. Leipzig has always been an important European trade center for durable goods and continues to maintain its reputation as the crossroads of the world's fur market. Although the practical East Germans prefer farm tractors to fur coats, they are not above catering to the profitable Western taste for dressing in the skins of animals.

Even when the fair is not in progress, there is much going on in this bustling metropolis. The State Theatre, center of the performing arts, charges the same nominal admission for every seat, and every seat is always filled. The long lines of music lovers queuing up at the box office around the clock testify to the cultural enthusiasm of this vibrant city. The theatre, like most buildings in the rebuilt center of town, is pleasingly functional. Karl Marx University, a modern skyscraper with a uniquely slanted roof, is fondly referred to by the students as "the wisdom tooth." Tuition, incidentally, is free to those who qualify.

The streets of Leipzig are not cluttered with traffic, and bicyclists and strollers are free to go about their business in peace and quiet. An efficient public transportation system, made up mainly of charming old streetcars, is a very popular way for the citizens of Leipzig to get around. And the people can move about in complete safety, secure in the knowledge that the vigilant Vopos are constantly watching out for them.

The Leipziger is fortunate not to be harassed by retailers hawking their wares at every turn. State shops offer him every necessity at modest prices and in modest surroundings. For those with foreign currencies, there are the State Intershops in which can be purchased every luxury item imaginable. These shops, however, attract mostly foreign visitors who, aside from being able to afford them, have not yet accustomed themselves to the simpler, more leisurely pace of this friendly town.

Although parishioners have let their churches fall into disrepair, the State has jumped in to keep Bach's historic St. Thomas Church available to foreign tourists. Faust's famous Auerbachs Keller also continues to be a popular tourist attraction. Elsewhere, Leipzigers are less interested in discos and more inclined to sip a local beer at a quiet Bierstube or spend a relaxed evening at home watching sports or speeches on the State television channels. Their children, not addicted to the tube, spend their evenings memorizing their lessons for school the next day.

So linger in lovable Leipzig, where the days seem like weeks. You'll feel better when you leave.

Exercise
What do you suppose Leipzig is really like? Examine the diction carefully to see where and how it misleads. Pick a town you know and promote it by using the tricks of the misleading style.

Example 3
Did you ever read a movie review, then see the movie, and wonder if you and the reviewer saw the same film? Movie reviews are essays of educated opinion at best, of rationalized bias at worst. The only time they are not misleading is when you agree with them. A movie reviewer eventually becomes either jaded or addicted, which gives you a choice between one who has lost his taste and one who has no taste at all. In rare instances, a reviewer may suffer from both extremes, in which case you may get something like this:

This latest film from Mason DeJoy, the courageous director who defied the courts to give the people honesty, is a new dimension in the art of *cinéma vérité*. *Pièce de Résistance* is so real you can smell the audience involvement in its gritty sense of place and its frontal assault on primal human emotions. At times its dominant imagery boldly thrusts its way into the viewer's psyche, insisting that its meaning be experienced firsthand. One sprawls in open-mouthed wonder before its relentless probing into the furthest recesses of man's (and woman's) innermost being. At times the action literally explodes on the screen.

Working with actors whose faces are as fresh as their language is frank, DeJoy has drawn out of them every ounce of talent they have to give. They are actors who do what they are hired to do. Act. When they feel, they feel; when they bore, they bore. Under DeJoy's supervision, they explore every nuance of reaction and response, deviating from their parts only in outbursts of consummate possession.

Without such frills as background music, lavish sets, costumes, DeJoy has reduced the film to its essence. In this masterpiece he holds the mirror (many mirrors) up to nature, letting people see themselves as they really are underneath. It is at once a celebra-

tion of the rites of passage and a holy mass of forgotten innocence. In the end, when one of the nurses searches desultorily
for her mislaid uniform, one is left wondering just what it is she
has lost.

In the lost and found of the human experience, so DeJoy seems
to be showing us, the true *pièce de résistance* is man's ability to
plunge ahead, to surmount any obstacle, to survive. Jack Hammer, an actor who is head and shoulders above most of the ac-
tresses in this film (remember him in *Stop the World, I Want to
Get Off?*) personifies this instinct for survival in his own inde-
fatigable performance. He is surely one of the few rising young
actors around these days with obvious staying power.

Unfortunately, this film will be seen, as most of DeJoy's films
have been, by none but a devoted following in those little out-
of-the-way converted art theatres so dear to the inner city. Most
major newspapers will probably not even advertise the film, let
alone review it. But hasn't that always been the fate of esoterica
in America? Put *Pièce de Résistance* on your must-see list and ignore its detractors who cannot see that this film is greater than
the sum of its private parts.

Exercise

You probably don't have to be told what kind of "flick" this one
is. And you probably don't have to have the *double-entendres*
spelled out for you. Have you ever seen "serious" films reviewed
in the same style? Can you pick out some of the commonplace
expressions likely to be found in reviews of obscure art films?
Write a movie review of your own in which you purposely mislead the reader into believing the film isn't what it really is.

Example 4

The press is constantly under attack for misleading the public.
Much of the attack is unfair. It is frequently leveled by persons
who would prefer to see their own distorted version of the news
put forth. A reporter has a hard time balancing biases and still
coming through with a story that satisfies both himself and the
reader and yet remains reasonably close to the facts. As observer,

interpreter, recorder, he is as much a part of what he perceives as the next man. Even so, there are those reporters who do get carried away occasionally, especially if they think they sniff foul play. The following account of a murder trial is by no means typical of most responsible court reporting these days, but it does demonstrate what used to happen—and still can happen—when a journalist becomes judge and jury.

On trial for the brutal slaying of her husband, community leader and philanthropist John Dough, his widow, Jane ("Baby") Dough broke down under Prosecuting Attorney Leo Lyon's brilliant cross-examination and confessed that she had once told her husband, "I'll see you burn in hell." The jury, obviously shocked at her coarseness, will not need long to reach a verdict in this case, exclaimed the triumphant prosecutor as he turned the witness over to her defense attorney, the notorious Yura Freeman.

Even Freeman, with his infamous skill at setting the guilty free, could not conceal the sordid facts of the case from a jury which has been ready, until now, to give Mrs. Dough every benefit of the doubt. They heard her admit that she came from a large, welfare-supported family, that she had longed to live in the exclusive part of town her husband came from, and that when Mr. Dough had proposed, she had found the offer (but not the man) irresistible. When asked about the speed of the marriage, she repeated her tedious story about the "false alarm."

She claimed she tried to be a good wife but that his family never gave her a chance. In spite of her testimony that his family had never accepted her, the jury heard reliable witnesses from the Dough family who swore that she rebuffed their every effort to make her acceptable to their circle of society.

Mrs. Dough insisted that she knew nothing of her husband's death until she found his bullet-riddled body floating face down in the swimming pool the morning after he had been shot. She claims she went to bed early the night before and slept soundly, without benefit of a sedative, although investigators testified that they found sleeping pills on her night stand. Her story is that her husband had been involved with some underworld characters who had been making threats on his life. When asked to be more explicit about this alleged involvement with criminals, Mrs. Dough pleaded understandable ignorance. It was her theory, nevertheless, that her husband had been shot somewhere else and later dumped into the pool. The state called this a "likely story" and asked for the death penalty.

Although the murder weapon has not yet been found, the state is convinced that the circumstances point "beyond the shadow of a reasonable doubt" to Dough's guilt. The victim's mother, and the state's primary character witness, described her son as a fine, upstanding boy who "never gave me a moment's worry." She went on to characterize Jane as a "fortune hunter" who "never knew how good she had it."

Recalled to the stand, Jane ("Baby") Dough told a tear-filled story of true love and insisted that she and her husband had got along very well, but neighbors testified to occasional arguments culminating in the shocking "see you in hell" threat.

If she is acquitted, Jane Dough stands to inherit a vast sum of money as well as most of the property and belongings of the deceased. This would come as a blow to those devoted members of the family who have remained so loyal to their wealthy son and brother in spite of his aloofness. As one irate brother put it, and with some justification: "If there was a hit man, he got the wrong person." Most observers agree, however, that the jury has no choice but to rectify that mistake.

Exercise

Can you sift the truth from the trappings in that account? What does the reporter emphasize? What does he omit? Does he introduce any irrelevancies, beg any questions, pander to any prejudices? Write a report of something you have witnessed (a meeting, a debate, an argument, an accident) and slant it so that your biases show.

Although it's fun to play around with it, the *misleading style* is no laughing matter. Careers have been ruined, characters assassinated through innuendo, falsification, and perhaps the most pernicious ploy of all, the suppression of crucial information. In our impatience with detail, our preference for headlines and news briefs, we are in constant danger of being misled. In our own eagerness to score a point or save face, we are apt to mislead. Whether by accident or by design, whether done poorly or done well, to write so as to mislead is to be guilty of the most insidious abuse of style of all.

14. The Diversionary Style

Being diversionary is merely verbal sleight-of-hand. The object is to distract your audience's attention from what you are really up to, to get them to look somewhere else while you fool them into believing what they see. You use this device when you do not want to answer a question directly or face an issue squarely. Usually, the reasons for such evasiveness are less than commendable: you don't know the answer, or you don't care to deal with the issue because the answer would not be well received. Sometimes, however, avoiding the main issue by directing attention elsewhere is the only way to withhold news that would inflict unnecessary pain on the recipient.

Here are some of the techniques of being diversionary:

1. stress minor points: give related issues disproportionate importance
2. minimize the main issue: give it a nod, then go on; shrug it off
3. get sidetracked: drag in "red herrings"
4. moralize: pontificate; sling mud
5. use questionable analogies, parallels, comparisons
6. use questionable statistics (or, at least, misleading ones)
7. beg the question: use two unproved statements to "prove" each other (Father's right because fathers know best)

After each of the following examples of the diversionary style, you will be asked to fill in what you think the real answer is that the writer would give to the initial question were he to confront the issue directly.

Example 1

Among the techniques peculiar to the diversionary style you will find some old friends, techniques you have been analyzing and imitating in previous chapters. Look for the use of "begging the question" and innuendo" in the following selection.

Question: How safe is a nuclear reactor?

A few hysterics equate nuclear reactors with atom bombs and see their home towns going up in mushroom clouds. Others, less hysterical but equally misguided, fear "melt down" and the contamination that would result from the release of radioactive gas. Still others worry that those living near nuclear plants might be subject to deadly exposure to radiation.

To begin with, nobody in the U.S. has been injured as a result of a commercial reactor accident since the first nuclear power plant went into operation twenty years ago. The odds are overwhelmingly against injury or death from reactor mishaps. The risk of dying as a result of an automobile accident is 75,000 times as high. Furthermore, people are exposed daily to radiation from other sources—coal-fired plants, color television, microwave ovens, X-rays—and never complain.

Where is the power for all our energy consumption to come from if not from the limitless resources of nuclear fusion and fission? If people insist on enjoying every modern convenience, they are going to have to accept the negligible risk of nuclear reactors. Life is never without risk. Most of us take chances daily—in cars, planes, bathtubs—that pose more of a threat to survival than reactors ever could. If Americans lag behind in nuclear power, less industrialized nations are going to catch up with and surpass us in technological advances and all that means to the perpetuation of the good life.

We should be too sophisticated these days to smash looms because of some irrational fear of progress. Only obstructionists, malcontents who protest for the sake of protest, can fail to see that nuclear reactors are a necessity if we are to improve the standard of living for everyone in this country. To reject nuclear power is to consign the have-nots to a lifetime of never having. We cannot afford such an elitist stance, either morally or economically. Don't ask how safe nuclear reactors are; ask how secure your future will be without them.

Answer: _____

Exercise

Go back to the second paragraph. What important things are left unsaid? Draw inferences. Examine the techniques of diversion and then try to incorporate them in your own diversionary nonanswer to one of the following question.

1. Is there really an energy shortage?
2. How economical is an economy car?
3. Are vitamin pills of any real value?

Example 2

The following selection raises an ethical question: how much risk do you admit in an operation that is the patient's only chance for recovery? Decide whether you think this approach is unjustly devious or justifiably diversionary.

Question: What are my chances of surviving this operation?

The only way to correct the blockage in your brain is to operate. Unless we operate, your condition will never improve. It might stabilize, or it might deteriorate, but it will never be what it was before the blockage occurred. It is a delicate operation, but then, so is every operation when you stop to think about it. Any tampering with the human body, any cutting through flesh and bone and inserting of foreign matter into the system is unnatural to the system and, therefore, risky. If some operations seem less delicate than others, it is simply because they are more common. People speak casually about appendectomies and hysterectomies and gall bladder operations only because they are not rare.

Because brain surgery sounds so exotic (what medical movie could get any glamour out of an appendectomy?), it also sounds perilous. There is something apparently more threatening about removing scalp hair than about shaving pubic hair. And even though the heart is the critical center of the body, it is the brain that gets more attention, maybe because it conjures up images of mad scientists and hunchbacked assistants transposing brains in cobwebby laboratories. Too many myths have grown up around brain surgery. About no other area of medicine is there so much popular ignorance and superstition; it's almost as if nobody wants to know much about it just as nobody really wants to talk about it. There seems to be something shameful about admitting that you've had brain surgery, as if you are inviting comments like "It's about time," or "Did they find anything?" The very idea that you may require brain surgery confirms people's suspicions about your sanity.

The operation we are proposing here is rare only because the malfunction is rare. In comparison with other types of brain surgery, it is actually a rather simple operation. The location of the blockage is easier to identify, which means less bone removal and less probing. Actual removal is the tricky part, but it has been accomplished more often than not. Even so, recovery is not guaranteed. However, patients who have not survived have usually suffered from other complications and not directly from the operation itself which has generally been successful.

Answer: _____

Exercise

Find any red herrings? any doubtful parallels? Pretend you feel obliged to be diversionary about the following questions. How would you go about it?

1. How safe is a motorcycle?
2. Can I get in and out of East Germany without any trouble?
3. Can I drink the water in Mexico?
4. What are my chances of passing this test?
5. How safe is the "pill"?

Example 3

In the following selection it is fairly easy to see which side the author takes. While he does seem to be answering the question, are his answers really answers or merely opinions?

Question: Are beauty contests sexist and racist?

The beauty contest is as American as apple pie. It is a tribute to the American woman, a gesture of respect for her virtues and a recognition of her pioneer spirit. American women have traditionally played strong roles in the formation of American values, and over the years they have emerged with a distinctive beauty made up of confidence, energy, and glowing health.

From the apple-cheeked young ladies of Massachusetts to the corn-fed lasses of Iowa to the golden girls of California, America has produced feminine beauty it can be proud of, and its beauty pageants are an expression of this pride. The girl who wins an American beauty contest is a far cry from the sexpot centerfold or the sultry siren. Her beauty is more than skin deep. It comes from a soul full of compassion, a heart full of love, and a mind alert and intelligent. These are good girls from wholesome backgrounds. These girls are bright, charming, and talented. And every one of them is vitally concerned about the problems of the world and intent on doing her part to solve them.

Those who view a beauty contest as a flesh market are those with prurient minds who look not at what a swimsuit reveals but dwell only on what it conceals. When these girls promenade in swimsuits, they are not flaunting their bodies but presenting for aesthetic appreciation the female human form as God created it. There is something pure and ennobling about this spectacle that the pure in spirit recognize and admire.

Some point out that beauty contestants are almost exclusively white, and that winners always are. Beauty is in the eye of the beholder, and judges cannot judge fairly if they are to look for anything but what they see. What they must see are qualities, not quotas; talent, not tokens. The beauty queen is the people's choice: she is of America, by America, and for America.

Answer: _____

Exercise

Analyze this selection carefully for side-tracking and question-able comparisons. Use the techniques of this diversionary an-swer to "answer" one of the following questions.

1. Are Protestants anti-Catholic?
2. Is most TV comedy moronic?
3. Is smoking hazardous to your health?

Example 4

In the following selection, notice how the main issue gets lost amid disproportionately stressed minor points. Notice, finally, how the terms are redefined.

Question: Is America's military strength inferior?

It has never been the American way to boast of its military might. In fact, historically, the U.S. has prepared itself for war only when the threat was imminent or the attack already mounted. In peacetime we have preferred to be a nation of peace, not stockpiling weapons in open invitation to other countries to doubt our word or fear our intentions.

We are not now at war, and although some say neither are we "at peace," we are certainly not under attack, nor is there any immediate threat to our national security from foreign or hostile forces. Nonetheless, for the past three decades we have had to increase our vigilance, especially in a world that has become con-stantly more fragile in its alliances and more inscrutable in its designs. Certain observers have made strong cases for the valid-ity of a real and present danger, although this danger is often more of a political nature than a military one. Others have re-minded us of our commitments to less defensible allies with whom we share certain interdependent freedoms. Because of cer-tain pledges we have made, we feel compelled to maintain ade-quate armaments and personnel to fulfill those pledges without hesitation. Of course, the degree of our preparedness depends on our estimate of the vulnerability of these weaker allies and on both their degree of danger and their ability to resist such danger themselves.

Military preparedness is not the same thing as military capability. Although we were not prepared for World War II, we demonstrated our capabilities swiftly. Military strength is a potential, not a fixed quantity. We have proved that we can mobilize the entire country if need be, but it would be pointless to do so now just to prove how tough we are. Even so, it's how tough we can be that counts. That's what military strength is. And in that regard, we are strong.

Answer: _____

Exercise

Be similarly diversionary in answering one or all of the following questions.

1. Is our team going to win the championship?
2. Is law protection reliable in this town?
3. Can I get a good education at this school?

Example 5

The issue of women reporters in men's locker rooms stirred a great deal of controversy a while back. What, precisely, is the issue being avoided in the following reply?

Question: Should women reporters be allowed in men's locker rooms?

The courts have ruled that women reporters are not to be barred from interviewing athletes in their (the athletes') locker rooms. Locker rooms are not ideal places to conduct interviews. They are steamy, smelly, noisy. The players are tired, sweaty, distracted. Their minds are on their bodies, not on the game. They want to shower and cool off and calm down. If they've won, they want to celebrate; and if they've lost, they want to commiserate.

A woman reporter who invades a men's locker room is not likely to have only sports on her mind. The sight of a gang of naked, sweaty jocks is hardly conducive to a level-headed interview. How is a woman going to listen to an answer and get it right while staring at a jock strap—or whatever? And how is an athlete going to know what he thinks—or conceal what he is thinking—when a woman is standing there gawking at his famous body? If she detects a mole on his left hip, will she report it? Will it influence her opinion of his playing? of the game?

Women say they are too professional to let male flesh bother them one way or the other. If that is true, what kind of women are they? Certainly the players' wives are not so "professional" that they can just stand by and let a lot of aggressive female reporters ogle their husbands. And what about the women reporters' husbands (assuming they've even got husbands)? Are they out for cheap thrills, too? Something to turn them both on later that evening?

You don't see male reporters panting to get inside women's locker rooms—although it would be perfectly understandable if they did. Invite women into the locker room today, and they'll be wanting to move in tomorrow.

Answer: _____

Exercise

The answer to the question posed in this paragraph may seem obvious at first, but if the real question has never been dealt with, then there can be no real answer. Write a response to one of the following questions that is so diversionary, the real question never gets fair treatment.

1. Should women be assembly line fore(men)?
2. Should men and women share public facilities?
3. Should a man have the right to decide whether or not his un-born child should be aborted?

There is a thin but crucial line between being discreet and being diversionary. If your honest purpose is to let someone down easily or stall for time because you know the cavalry is on the way, then you are being discreet and your intentions are honorable. But if you try to dodge a painful issue or cover up a wrongdoing because you know the truth would get you in trouble, then you are guilty of being diversionary and your intentions are not honorable. Even if you are merely trying to conceal your own ignorance and protect your feelings, it is better to be silent than to be sneaky about it.

15. The Imitative Style

Imitation is more than flattery; it's a way of life. Much as we may long for more pizzazz in business or scientific writing, the truth is that few would survive in those worlds if their memos or lab reports were "creative." While there may be room for imagination at the top, junior executives and assistant researchers know that it's safest to sound like everybody else. If they could get away with it, they'd clip words out of newspapers and paste them together so that no one could trace their prose. It can be comforting to have a language uniform to hide in.

Not long ago a university vice-president wrote a flippant memo to a psychology professor in which he used words like "shrink" and phrases like "get your head together"—all in jest. The professor didn't think the memo was funny at all and sued the vice-president for harassment. You can well imagine that today his memos are "fool" proof.

"Better safe than sorry" is the hackneyed slogan of the imitative writer. If there is anything to be learned from his style, it is how easy it is for even the strongest willed to lapse into copy-cat prose. If you know how it's done, then perhaps you can keep from doing it—if you want to. If you don't want to, if you don't dare to be different, then here's your ticket to merry mediocrity.

Although the essence of the imitative style is slavish imitation of the particular kind of writing you want to copy—and this varies from profession to profession—there are a few techniques common to all varieties.

1. use jargon: each profession has its cherished diction, and mastering it is the first rule of imitation
2. use clichés: time-worn phrases are great for those spaces between jargon words
3. use the passive voice: cover yourself; cover your sources ("It has been noted . . ." "It has been brought to my attention . . .")
4. be impersonal: be referee, not participant; be detached, aloof, icy
5. use routine diction: beyond jargon and clichés are loads of lackluster words that leave no impression
6. be sober: don't pun; don't parody; avoid irony, satire, wit of any kind; be dull
7. be solemn: act as if you mean what you say
8. be colorless: don't give them something they can pin on you; don't embellish; write perishable prose

Example 1
Police reports are almost accidentally ironic. Their heavy-handed style amounts to understatement when you realize the drama it conceals.

The officer on duty was apprised of the alleged attempt at illegal entry and was dispatched to the address given. Said officer arrived at the scene where the suspect was observed effecting entry into the building. The officer instructed the suspect to cease and desist, whereupon said suspect departed the scene on foot. The officer then proceeded to pursue the suspect and apprehended him three blocks away after a brief exchange of gunfire. The officer then took the suspect into custody, confiscated his weapon, and recited to him his rights. Thereupon, said officer proceeded to escort said suspect to police headquarters, whereupon the suspect was duly interrogated and then incarcerated.

Exercise

What jargon is present in this paragraph? Can you reconstruct the scene more vividly? Try using the same style to report the interrogation of this suspect.

Example 2

Public relations is the growth industry of modern times. Corporations have staffs who do nothing but smooth ruffled feathers and soothe savage breasts. Small-business owners have to do their own PR work, but they have been quick to borrow a page from their bigger brothers.

I am in receipt of your letter of May 2 in which you complain about the service you received in this restaurant recently. My associates and I appreciate having your opinion and regret that you were inconvenienced. Our first consideration has always been the satisfaction of our customers. We want them to feel comfortable and enjoy themselves. Whenever anything interferes with this goal, we do our best to remedy the situation.

Rest assured that your complaint has not gone unattended. Steps have already been taken to see that no customer is ever neglected again. The waitress in question has been reprimanded and has asked me to offer you her apologies. We have also reminded all members of our staff that it has always been our policy to put the customer first.

We hope you will give us the privilege of allowing us to welcome you once again to our restaurant. We are proud of our reputation and wish to maintain it. The management would be honored if you would accept the enclosed guest certificates entitling you and a companion to a complimentary dinner at your convenience.

If we can be of any further service, please do not hesitate to let us know.

Exercise

Can you pick out the jargon? identify the clichés? indicate the routine diction? Is the tone sober and sincere? What is the writer really thinking? Write a letter in which you handle a customer complaint of a different kind. Make your style as bland and innocuous as you can.

Example 3

Sociologists are notorious for their jargon. There are those who suspect that success in the field depends almost exclusively on one's ability to master its arcane language. Here is a sociologist's report of a poor child caught between family and friends.

The socio-economic factors affecting this case are in evidence in every aspect of the formative-evaluative process. The peer-sibling pressure ratio demonstrates a marked imbalance in favor of group response preference. However, the environmental stress index reveals a continuance pattern suggesting severe extrapersonal threats on standard heterogeneous tendencies resulting in demonstrable damage to the normal homogeneous-heterogeneous tension balance personality level. Similar symptoms of personality deprivation are manifest in the results of the pecuniary restrictions and fluctuations register, the preferred alternative to the Pinot necessity-luxury survival indicator now considered ineffective in cases of extreme regression and persistent alienation when contradictory influences are operative.

Exercise

Unless you plan to become a sociologist, don't even bother to try to imitate this style. You might, however, look for similar gobbledygook in a sociology textbook you haven't yet sold back to the bookstore. What words have the sociologists borrowed from the psychologists?

Example 4

Educators are also jargon junkies—and with less excuse. They are particularly addicted to using nouns as adjectives, and the more noun-adjectives they can string together, the higher they get. See if you can figure out what is going on in this paragraph. Hyphenation might help.

The competency core teacher performance student response learning equivalency acquisition orientation absorption function ascendancy evaluation scale has proved effective in making modern educators more aware of norm distribution alertness expectations within deviancy control comprehension awareness curriculum stimulus statistics consciousness programs.

Exercise
Try reading the whole paragraph aloud without taking a breath.

Example 5
Routine office-memo jargon is not unclear; it is merely trite. When it becomes offensive is when people who should know better lapse into this style.

Please be advised that the item you ordered is now in our warehouse. Will you advise as to disposition of this item as soon as possible as delivery may be delayed. A memo to this effect (attached) is included with this letter. Please read and return to this office.

Exercise
Notice the overuse of "advise" (which has nothing to do with advice) and the conjunction "as." Also notice how the fondness for parentheses leads to redundancy. The last sentence is a classic. "Return to this office" sounds like an order to go back and see the boss again. What examples of "office-ese" have you come across?

Example 5
Higher up the office ladder are those officials who love to couch bad news in highbrow jargon. See if you can figure out the point of this directive.

Financial exigencies mandate a realignment of budgetary priorities. Pursuant to company policy, stringent restrictions on unwarranted expenditures will take effect immediately. Anticipated monetary liabilities will also entail readjustment of salary increment projections for the forthcoming fiscal year.

Exercise
Feel the pinch? This might be a good style to use when you're trying to fend off a creditor. Write a similar paragraph in which you haul out the big words in order to tell someone you can't pay up.

Example 6
The letter of reprimand is a touchy one. Since it could easily lead to the filing of a grievance or even a lawsuit, many of those unfortunate enough to have to write such a letter find it discreet to fall back upon a well-used format. Notice the use of clichés and routine diction. Also notice how the recipient is given the chance to get himself off the hook.

It has come to my attention that you have not been meeting your classes regularly. Far be it from me to interfere with your academic freedom, but it is my responsibility to superintend the quality of the program. As you know, it is a matter of policy at this university that instructors adhere to their contractual obligations and perform their duties in accordance with prescribed regulations. If there has been some misunderstanding, I should be more than happy to discuss it with you. Please feel free to make an appointment at your convenience to come in and talk this over. If there have been extenuating circumstances, I would appreciate being made cognizant of them.

If I do not hear from you, I will assume that the situation has been remedied and that you are meeting your classes on a regular basis.

Exercise
Write a letter in which you smack somebody's wrist. Use as many of the standard phrases from the above letter as you can. Can you think of any others that are commonly used in such a case?

Example 7

Students of literature are about the cagiest imitators around. For whatever reasons (and there are some good ones), it doesn't take long for them to lapse into journal jargon and write "scholarly" papers that are easily distinguishable from the prose they analyze. The following article is admittedly a parody, but it's hard to avoid parody when writing about literature. In it you will find most of the trademarks of uninspired, unoriginal literary style. In this case, also look for routine methods of establishing the premise as well as of defending it.

Generations of scholars have misread Joseph Conrad's *Heart of Darkness*, most of them preferring to identify the "heart" with the "self" and the "darkness" with "nothingness." Patterson, it is true, has postulated a core of hope; and Anderson has written at length about the "return to instinct" represented by Kurtz and his abandonment to his libido. Murray has even gone a step further (over the edge?) and labored the tantalizing premise that man is actually capable of losing his instincts, of becoming non-human in an alien environment. These, and many others, are interesting footnotes to Conrad's challenging novella, but no one has yet seemed ready to confront the central issue: just what is the "heart" of "darkness"?

We know of Conrad's love of the English language and the word play in which he takes such delight. Surely, when he wrote "heart," his mind's eye saw "hart." In a letter to Jacob Stanley, written only a short time after completion of *Heart of Darkness*, Conrad says, in speaking of a return visit to the Scottish highlands, that it is a place "the *hart* (my italics) would take flight in" (his preposition). He did insert an "e" above a caret, thus revising "hart" to read "heart," but if he had truly wanted to eliminate the double meaning, why did he not simply cross out "hart" entirely and write "heart" in above it? There is good reason to assume that when Conrad wrote "heart" in *Heart of Darkness*, he saw a symbolic deer, nervous and alert, vital and vulnerable, thrust into an alien jungle the way the heart is thrust into despair. Thus, the stag, symbol of purity, of the solitary life, of fleetness, is Kurtz thrust into the soul's dark night, sinless Kurtz a solitary man, succumbing swiftly to the overpowering forces of darkness.

Why Conrad chose "darkness" instead of, say, "despair" or "hell" or "hopelessness" has long puzzled scholars. Some say it is misleading and refuse to wrestle with it. Others argue that its meaning is as murky as the word implies and prefer to leave it that way. Such evasions are a dereliction of the scholar's duty. We cannot assume that Conrad was a careless artist who threw words together in a slapdash manner—especially titles! He knew what he was doing, and there is solid evidence to prove that he did.

Although he makes no reference to her in the novella itself, Conrad has mentioned elsewhere his fascination with the sainted Maid of Orleans. He records somewhere that as a child he doted on the lives of the saints, and although Joan of Arc was not canonized until much later, Conrad must have known that she was ineluctably slated for the honor. It is easy to understand why Conrad would have remained devoted to this enigmatic girl, this incorruptible Jeanne d'Arc. She, like Kurtz, came from the sunlight of a happy childhood into the twilight of war and intrigue and then finally into the midnight of torture and humiliation, excommunication and death. Were they not both objects of scorn? Did not both die exalted within, debased from without? Did they not, at the moment of death, see the same "horror" around them? It is into Jeanne's kind of "d'Arc-ness" that Kurtz is absorbed, and it is her kind of victory he wins in the heart of Marlowe who preserves his sanctity with a holy lie, a higher truth.

Kurtz is the mutilated stag upon the faggots. Surely he would have been sacrificed on those heathen fires just as Joan was sacrificed on those "holy" fires had not Marlowe "rescued" him. I think Joan, had she been so snatched from the flames only to linger and die in prison, might have uttered the same desperate condemnation of man's inhumanity to man: "The horror, the horror!"

Perhaps Kurtz was even thinking of her as he voiced that pained exclamation. In his German accent maybe he was really saying: "The whore, the whore!" After all, it was Shakespeare himself who called her slut, and we know that Conrad read Shakespeare. And which "brutes" would he have wanted "exterminated" if not those nasty inquisitors who burned his darling "whore-saint" at the stake?

Exercise
First analyze, then refute, then avoid.

We tend to be curiously ambivalent about imitation. On the one hand we deplore it saying that it stifles creativity; on the other we lapse into it frequently because often we think it "sounds" right. Business letters have a ring to them, scholarly articles have a ring to them, legal documents have a decided ring to them; and it's easy for us to deceive ourselves into thinking that our writing is better than it is when it, too, has a ring to it. Furthermore, people who read other people's attempts at writing (teachers, editors, friends) often base their evaluations on how closely what they read conforms to what they expect, and their expectations are based on the "ringing" they hear from what they have read before. It's one thing to demand originality or attempt it; it's another to be confident enough to recognize it or pursue it. Maybe this chapter has given you the incentive, if not the confidence, both to recognize it and to pursue it.

16. The Confessional Style

The Gut and Gush School of Writing is now open for business. Here's your chance, at last, to do what you've been dying to do ever since you were a sophomore in high school—let it all hang out. In this chapter you won't get slapped on the wrist for using "I" or for writing fragments or using slang or underlining words you want to emphasize or putting exclamation points after particularly pithy phrases. In fact, the subject matter of this chapter is "I," and whatever "I" want to say about "myself" is nobody's business but *my own*. So *there!*

After all, life *is* a subjective experience, and we *are* a part of what we perceive. What, then, could be more honest than to be totally impressionistic about absolutely everything? Unfortunately, it isn't that simple. With rare exceptions, confessional writing is the most dishonest writing of all. Even Rousseau, in his famous *Confessions,* found this out. When he criticized others, he seemed waspish; when he criticized himself, he seemed masochistic; and when he defended himself, he seemed either petulant or proud. The trouble is that it is extremely difficult for a reader to read a confession and maintain a consistent perspective. He is forced either to abandon his critical faculty and identify wholly with the confessor or to exercise his critical faculty ruthlessly and pass judgment on the confessor.

Compassion or contempt are the reader's choices, and neither is conducive to balanced appreciation. Ultimately it comes down to this: Why is this person telling on himself? That's the question that nags at us as we read a confession. And since there is never a satisfactory answer to it, we are left feeling uncomfortable, even embarrassed.

Nevertheless, confessional writing abounds, and we all have as much of a taste for reading it as we do for writing it. The urge to share confidences is elemental. The fact that it won't get us very far (even as therapy, it's questionable) doesn't have to bother us as long as we know that confessional writing is an exercise done for its own sake. The problem is: how forthright can we really be about ourselves? Is it possible to be truthful about ourselves? Do we really know what the truth is? Assuming we do, why are we telling it? Keep these questions in mind as you work through the examples that follow. Notice how you are inexorably tempted to read between the lines, to be aware more of what the writer is concealing than of what he is revealing.

Here are the techniques of the confessional style. If they seem to border on the fraudulent, it is simply because fraud is an inextricable part of confession, like it or not.

1. use first person: be preoccupied with yourself
2. use phrases like "I'm the sort of person who . . ."
3. tell jokes on yourself
4. exalt or humiliate yourself
5. be sentimental
6. be shameless
7. be dishonestly honest, frank, candid
8. psychoanalyze yourself
9. compare yourself with oddballs
10. confess imaginary sins or crimes

Example 1
Test your reactions to the following boast. How detached can you remain? how sympathetic?

If you want to know the truth, I got through college without ever cracking a book. You want to know how I did it? I had a system, that's how. First, I'd psych out the prof. If it was some young chick just out of grad school, no sweat. I'd sit there in about the third row and just ogle her. At first it would turn her off, but eventually she'd start writing me notes. I mean, she'd say things on my papers like "Better see me" or "I do have office hours, you know." Sure, I knew. But I also knew that it was smart to hold out until just about three or four weeks before finals. Then I'd saunter in—and boy, the way she'd clear out whoever else was in there and make room for me. First she'd play it cool—maybe glasses and the whole bit. Tell me how poor a record I had of passing, how I hadn't a prayer—without her help, of course. Of course! That's what I'm here for, I'd say, and play the regenerate sinner. Then I'd slowly lay on her all the "problems" I'd been having, and pretty soon she'd be right up there, all ears (and eyes) and tea and sympathy. Maybe something could be done. When we'd agreed it could, I'd back off, let her wonder, let her sweat, then string her along until by finals she wouldn't know where she was coming from. But she'd come across with that grade—"A" if she was really turned on, "B" if she was confused. I used to wonder how she felt later, sitting there in her office all day, just waiting for me to show up and be grateful, so that she could tell me how generous she'd been. Only I wouldn't show up. No way. Wonder how she felt. Wonder if she's still sitting there, waiting.

If the prof was some old geezer, I'd get around to his office some day and play prodigal son. It never fails to get to them. I mean, that's what they're in the business for—to play mommy and daddy to the children of the world, always looking for that ideal child they thought they'd have if they married another prof— but somehow it just didn't work out that way. So this old guy's got a jerk for a son who's making it rough on the old man's image, and here I come along and play the regenerate again, only in a different key, and he's *forcing* the "A" on me, swallowing all my garbage about how great the course is and he is and how I just want to pass and all that and he's telling me that I'm a diamond in the rough and he's giving me my big chance.

But it's the tests that are the easiest. Nobody in his right mind could flunk an objective test. Everybody knows that if the answers are long and complicated, they're true. They're like crossword puzzles—a little guesswork here, a little cheating there, and you've got it made. And as for essays, well, they're even easier if you don't even try to pretend you know anything. Just breeze along, shoveling it out, buttering up the prof's prejudices, sounding stupidly wise one moment, wisely stupid the next. Of course, you've got to have brains not to have to have brains, if you know what I mean. It's the smarts that count. It also helps to have a studious girlfriend and a good fraternity file. And charm!

Exercise

How much stock do you put in this confession? Analyze the sentence structure. What effect does it have on this "snow job"? Write a similarly boastful confessional on one of the following topics.

1. I never exercise
2. I'm irresistible
3. I've never been to college, but . . .

Example 2

The self put-down is a common brand of confession. How sorry is the writer of this selection for the way he says he is?

I'm one of those persons who just can't cope. No matter what I try my hand at, I fail miserably. I don't know what's wrong with me, but I guess that's just the way I am. Sometimes I remind myself of one of those screwball comedians who's always lighting a match in a gas-filled room or stepping out onto a balcony that isn't there. Give me a job to do and I'll mess it up. Give me an important message to deliver and I'll blow it. Ask me a favor, and you'll never ask me again. If you've got me for a friend, you don't need an enemy.

Basically, I don't mean to be such a misfit. Basically, I want to do the right thing by everybody. I want to be liked—no, loved. Maybe I try too hard. Like the time this lady asked me to help her change a tire. I wanted to help her—poor thing—stranded there by the side of the road, all dressed up and staring at this dumb flat tire like a donut with a chunk bitten out of it. What did I do? I set the jack at an angle, and when the tire came off, the car came crashing down on her arms. (You don't think *I* was going to put *my* hands under there, do you?) So there she was, jumping up and down and screaming about how, if she didn't have two broken arms, she'd clobber me with the lug wrench. I got the hell out of there and got to the nearest phone to call for help. But I didn't have any change, and how was I to know about a free operator? When I got back to her and saw all those people crowded around, I figured the best thing was just to take off. So off I took, and here I sit, guilty conscience and the whole scene, wondering if she'll ever return my lug wrench, the bitch!

No, honestly, I worry about things like that. I believe in friendship. You know, "If you're ever up a tree, call on me." Well don't. Because once I was called on to help a fellow out of a tree, and he didn't appreciate it. I even got a ladder and propped it up and everything, and then he blamed me when the ladder slipped and he fell and broke a shoulder. Don't look a gift horse in the mouth, said I, but he said he'd take care of my mouth the day he got out of a cast. He even said something about me belonging in a tree, but you wouldn't catch me up in one of those things for love or money. Well maybe for love. I've never been too lucky in that ballpark, either. Somehow I always end up being accused of having sharp elbows or icy fingers or corkscrew toenails.

What a bundle of misery am I! I'd write to Dear Abby, but every time I lick a stamp, it sticks to my tongue. Why was I born? I don't even want to know.

Exercise

Write a similar "sob story" based on one of the following suggestions.

1. I'm a loser
2. I'm a bastard
3. I'm not well
4. I'm a slob
5. I can't boil water (open the hood)

Example 3

Some people act as if they have a franchise on life that sets them apart from the rest of us colorless slobs. The older they get, the more relentlessly young they are determined to stay. Is the writer of the following confession trying to convince you or herself?

I love life, and I love to be with young people because they are so full of life. They always tell me I may be old in years but I'm young at heart. And I always say you're only as old as you feel. And I feel young, young, young! Oh, life is such a challenge! Every morning I wake up eager to face it, reminding myself that today is the first day of the rest of my life. I'm just bursting with plans. I'm going to paint and write and learn to play the dulcimer and practice yoga and maybe even join the Peace Corps. Don't laugh. They love people my age. They know we have so much to offer—a lifetime of experience just waiting to be shared. Oh what I could teach those Indians along the Amazon, those islanders in the South Pacific, those poor blacks in Africa.

Let me have little children about me. I don't mind their squeals, their pranks, their messes. They are the light of the world, and I suffer them to come unto me, for out of the mouths of babes come blessings that passeth understanding. Some call children ungrateful, but that is not true. Maybe they accept something as if they have it coming to them, but that is only because they *do.* Youth will be served. The world is theirs, and we must give it to them. It is we who are false, for we say "thank you" with insincerity in our voices and a dishonest smile upon our faces. I do not want their thanks. They know that I enjoy giving almost as much as they enjoy receiving. It is I who should be grateful.

I should thank them for welcoming me into their lives and sharing with me their troubles and their dreams. If only my own son and daughter had opened their arms to me and accepted me as a friend. Instead, they scoff and tell me to act my age. *Act, hah!* I don't put on an act for anyone. Let them think what they will, go where they like. As I always told them, someday, when they have children of their own, then they'll understand the importance of becoming as a little child.

We have a choice here in life. We can either grow old or grow up. If I refuse to grow old, am I refusing to *grow* up? No, I am refusing to *give* up. So turn up the rock and take back the rocking chair. Life, here I come!

Exercise
Imitate this type of confession by applying it to one of the following suggestions:

1. I love people
2. I love my work
3. I love to love

Example 4
The taskmaster is often a proud person who believes he is leading when he is really showing off. He will knock himself out just to prove that everybody else is lazy. Worst of all, he flatters himself that he does what he does for righteousness' sake. Witness the following:

I don't demand anything of anybody else that I don't demand of myself. As far as I'm concerned, we're all in this together, and each of us pulls his own weight. I realize that different people are capable of different things, but if we're all going to get an equal share of the pie, then I think we should carry an equal share of the load. If I seem sometimes to drive others hard, it's only because I think I drive myself even harder. I could flatter myself that I have more endurance, but I'm inclined to think that the truth of the matter is that so many others simply have less drive. They could all do as much as I do, I'm sure, if they'd only put their minds—and their shoulders—to it.

Work is not competition, it's cooperation. A team of oxen won't get a plow through a swamp by fighting with each other. What we've got to do is pull together, equally, sharing the burden, distributing it fairly, working in unison toward a common goal. I like to think that the laborer is worthy of his hire, and if he is one of my laborers, well, he damn well better prove that he is worthy or hightail it out of here. I don't hold with slacking off when there's a job to be done. I've had my fill of goof-offs and goldbricks in my time, and I know how to deal with them.

When I lead, I expect people to follow. If they can't catch up, well they're better off left behind. But don't let them come knocking at my door for a hand out. I say, if you can't cut it, then cut out. Shape up or ship out. Put up or shut up. Nobody ever died of honest work. This country was built on hard work, and hard work's the only way anybody ever made anything of himself. I'm proud of what I've made of myself, and I owe it all to hard work. I'd rather wear out than rust out.

Work, saith the Lord, for the night is coming. So get off your can and get on the stick. There's no rest for the wicked, and we were born sinners and we're going to die sinners. There's no rest in hell, either, so follow me on the long hard path to glory. And when we get there, if it's rest you're after, don't ask me, ask the Old Man.

Exercise

How many clichés can you identify in this selection? How do you account for them? Write a similarly bombastic confessional on one of the following ideas.

1. I don't expect people to love me, just obey me.
2. Do as I say, not as I do.
3. I cannot abide a bore.

Example 5

The "Apologia pro Vita Sua" is the kind of confession only a John Henry Cardinal Newman can do justice to. Most "apologies" become orgies of shame or smugness. It's hard to avoid being vulgar when you are washing your dirty linen in public. Notice how the following confession reeks with hypocrisy which, as Rochefoucauld observed, is the homage that vice pays to virtue.

I've done some shameful things in my life, but I'm not about to get down on my knees to anybody. Why should I? Nobody's perfect. And I'm sure there are loads of people who've done a lot worse things than I've ever done—or ever dreamed of doing. Not to mention those people who *say* they've never done a bad thing in their lives—or those miserable people who really honestly haven't! Think what torment they must be going through, wishing they had, envying those who have, wondering if it's too late, despising everybody who's ever "lived."

I haven't got time to sit around regretting the things I've done. If I turned against my friends, that's my business. They probably weren't friends anyway, or they'd have turned the other cheek. You never know a true friend until you turn against him. And that guy who left his wife for me just before I threw him over: obviously a creep who'd do that to one woman would do it to another. I just wasn't taking any chances. Besides, I was doing his wife a favor. She should've thanked me instead of taking me to court. What a rotten thing to do, dragging my reputation through the mud, not that there wasn't plenty of mud to drag it through. But I'll say one thing, I keep my dirt under the carpet. It wasn't my idea to broadcast it to the world. It was hers! I ought to put out a contract on her.

But I would never do that. I wouldn't hurt a fly. I might hate her, but I'd never hurt her. Because of her I can't get a "decent" job anywhere. It doesn't bother me the way I'm forced to earn my money, but it sure bugs the hell out of my kids. That nosy PTA's always wanting to know what mommy does for a living. You call that a living? They tell her I'm an Avon lady. Well, I do ring doorbells, but I'm not common. I've been known to say no— and mean it. "Let your aye mean aye and your nay mean nay," my mother always taught me, and that's about all she taught me. At lot of men have learned more at my knee than I ever learned at hers.

No, I'm no scarlet woman. I'm just a pink lady (ha, ha!). Jesus loves me, that I know, 'cause Billy Graham told me so. And I'm getting me one of those fancy mansions just waiting for me up there in the sky. Right now, though, I've got me some slimming down to do if I'm ever going to squeeze through the eye of that blasted needle. Needle? Aw, come on now.

Exercise

Inimitable, you say? It's reminiscent of the Moll Flanders style. Try your hand at it. The trick is to be both sorry and smug at the same time. Remember, there's a quality of vanity in any confession. See what you can do with one of the following suggestions.

1. If I didn't do it, somebody else would.
2. So what if I don't always practice what I preach.
3. I could tell you some hairy stories.
4. My intentions are always good.
5. It's not how good you are but how long you last that counts.

A "true confession," as you can see, is by and large a contradiction in terms. Confessions are probably the most blatant manipulations of everything from the facts to the reader's sympathies. They make a fool of both writer and reader, but what willing fools we often are. Probably their appeal lies in the fact that most of us like to talk about ourselves as much as we like to hear intimate things about others. Whatever the impulse, the style of the confession is best left to gossip columnists and Hollywood has-beens.

V

Traditions

The English language as we know it hasn't been around for long. Columbus had already discovered America well before anyone was writing the sort of English prose we can easily read today. And few back then would have been willing to bet that the English they wrote in would survive half as long as it has. You would think now that Shakespeare's achievements would have put such misgivings to rest once and for all, but less than a century after him, John Milton was worrying that writing in English might well be a one-way ticket to oblivion.

Fortunately for us, English has survived pretty much intact since the Renaissance, affording us a marvelous opportunity to study and appreciate and profit from a stylistic tradition that spans five centuries. In this section a separate chapter is devoted to the dominant prose style of each of these centuries. First you will encounter the labyrinthine structures and mellifluous cadences of

179

the Baroque Style of the sixteenth century, after which you will
discover the vigorous, practical Senecan Style of the seventeenth
century. Then you will dabble in the elegances of the Augustan
Style of the eighteenth century, delve into the earnestness of the
Victorian Style of the last century, and arrive at last at the insou-
ciance that characterizes the style of much of the prose of this
century.

In matters of style, nothing is sacred. An irreverent attitude
toward the past is the only way to keep from becoming either
blinded or bored by it. You cannot write an imitation that will
do you or your style any good while you are holding your breath
in awe. Better to parody than to parrot the models that you find
set before you. If imitation is the highest form of flattery, surely
parody is the highest form of imitation.

Since there is nothing more deadly dull than trying to imitate
a paragraph or even a sentence that looks like a paragraph or a
sentence, just lying there in a lump, defying dissection, you will
find that most of the models in this section have been written in
a format that resembles (but only resembles) free verse. This
means that sentence elements such as clauses, phrases, com-
pounds, parallels, and series have already been identified for you
and written on separate lines to make analysis much simpler and
imitation (or parody) a great deal easier and far more meaningful.

Ernest Hemingway used to consciously compete with the masters of the past, taking on Flaubert one year, Tolstoy the next,
not always winning but usually thinking he won. Now it's your
turn. As you acquaint (or reacquaint) yourself with the proud
tradition of English prose style, not only are you bound to learn
a lot from those who have already gone through what you're going
through now, but—who knows?—you may even take a few of
them on and end up going some of them one better.

17. The Baroque Style

By the sixteenth century, English had abandoned its cumbersome Anglo-Saxon grammar and syntax and had absorbed the elegances of French into a language that we recognize today as having the sight and sound, the grace and cadence, of Modern English. While it retained much of the earthiness of Old English, it had acquired that flexibility of vocabulary and sentence structure that has allowed it to accommodate endless change and still remain essentially the same.

With the introduction of the printing press into England in the late fifteenth century, writers gained more confidence in English as a living, enduring language, and they took increasing delight in the manipulation of a language still relatively free of fixed and stifling rules. To them it was as if they had suddenly come upon a new and wonderful toy, a lute perhaps, newly arrived from Italy, rich in harmonious possibilities; and they orchestrated its sounds and rhythms as if they were writing sonatas rather than sermons. This is the style we know as Baroque—convoluted, extravagant, gorgeous—and the more gorgeous it got, the more inclined were its practitioners to favor sound over sense. What impresses us most today is the obvious zest with which they tackled whatever matter happened to be at hand. The joy of their endeavors comes through even the most tortuous prose of the period. They saw in this emerging language enormous opportunities for new ways of expressing themselves, and they seized upon these opportunities with a passion that reached its height in the astonishing verbal fireworks of William Shakespeare.

As in all ages, the best minds applied themselves to the medium of most immediate challenge. Everyone was excited by what could be done with an instrument they had been taking for granted, even apologizing for. Suddenly English was shown as capable of doing what Latin and French could do—and more. Though few could read, those few demanded that their minds be teased. Those who had access to theatres crowded into them, hungry for the flourishes and embellishments that would puzzle their minds one moment, dazzle them the next, and dazzle as they puzzled. And for those who could not attend plays, there was always the church where impassioned orators delivered the message of God and glory, fire and brimstone in language which thrilled while it threatened, cheered even as it challenged. In an age lacking in most of the diversions we take for granted, language was high entertainment.

The rhetoricians of the sixteenth century had elaborate formulas by which to construct their prose. They followed carefully prescribed rules for the use of balance, antithesis, symmetry, inclusion of proverbs and examples, and the use of figurative language. Generally, they built their sentences and paragraphs on the model of Cicero, to which they added certain original touches. It has always been in the nature of English, however, to burst the bonds of formality and take on a distinct life of its own. The writers of the sixteenth century rebelled even as they wrote, and this revolutionary spirit has remained a healthy element of the language right down to the present day.

The adjective "euphuistic," meaning "affectedly elegant," comes from the sixteenth century romance, *Euphues,* by John Lily. The following paragraph is from a section of that work entitled "The Anatomy of Wit."

Gentlewoman, my acquaintance being so little,
    I am afraid my credit will be less,
    for that they commonly are soonest believed,
    that are best beloved,
    and they liked best,
    whom we have known longest,
    nevertheless the noble mind suspecteth
    no guile without cause,
    neither condemneth any wight without proof,
    having therefore notice of your heroical heart,
    I am the better persuaded of my good hap.
For as the hop the pole being never so high groweth to
the end,
    or as the dry beech kindled at the root,
    never leaveth until it come to the top,
    or as one drop of poison disperseth itself into every
    vein,
    so affection having caught hold of my heart,
    and the sparkles of love kindled my liver,
    will suddenly though secretly flame up into my head,
    and spread itself into every sinew.
It is your beauty (pardon my abrupt boldness), lady,
    that hath taken every part of me prisoner,
    and brought me unto this deep distress,
    but seeing women when one praiseth them for their
    desserts,
    deem that he flattereth them to obtain his desire,
    I am here present to yield myself to such trial,
    as your courtesy in this behalf shall require.

Here is a modern imitation of this passage, addressed this time
not to a fickle lady but to a fickle employer:

Sir, my experience being so little,
    I am afraid my standing will be less,
    for that they usually are first fired,
    that are last hired,
    and they let go last
    who joined up earliest,

nevertheless the fair mind suspects not without cause,
neither blames any worker without proof,
having therefore notice of your generous heart,
I am the better persuaded of my chances.
For as the vine the tree being never so high grows to
the top,
or as the tree stump kindled at the root,
never stops burning until the stump is consumed,
or as one drop of dye disperses itself throughout the
vat,
so hunger having caught hold of my stomach,
and the fear of it dizzied my brain,
will suddenly and cruelly gnaw at my belly,
and spread itself into every entrail.
It is your generosity (pardon my abrupt boldness), sir,
that has given me hope,
and brought me unto this high expectation,
but seeing employers when one praises them for their
kindness,
deem that he flatters them to obtain his desire,
I am here present to submit myself to such tests,
as your goodness in this behalf shall require.

Exercise

Write a paragraph in imitation of the euphuistic style. The following topics may help you get started.

1. asking for a refund
2. asking for a change of grade
3. asking for a loan (grant, scholarship)

Here is a paragraph of Baroque prose that is much less euphuistic
than the paragraph from Lily. It is from Richard Hooker's *Of the
Laws of Ecclesiastical Polity* (The Law of Nature), and it inclines
in the direction of the more straightforward style of the seventeenth century, particularly after the first sentence. The first sentence, however, which is 200 words long, can be called nothing
if not "gorgeous." It is an incredible example of a *periodic* sen-

tence. Notice how the suspense builds as the "if" clauses strike all major chords on their way to that final climactic question. Notice, also, how the tension of such a lengthy sentence is relieved by the shorter, simpler sentences that follow. And notice that when the point of the paragraph is finally made in the last sentence, when the long question is finally answered, the important thought comes in a concluding "if" clause.

Now if Nature should intermit her course and leave altogether, though it were but for a while, the observation of her own laws;

if those principal and mother elements of the world, whereof all things in this lower world are made, should lose the qualities which they now have;

if the frame of that heavenly arch erected over our heads should loosen and dissolve itself;

if celestial spheres should forget their wonted motions and by irregular volubility turn themselves any way as it might happen;

if the prince of the lights of heaven which now as a giant doth run his unwearied course, should as it were through a languishing faintness begin to stand and to rest himself;

if the moon should wander from her beaten way,

the times and seasons of the year blend themselves by disordered and confused mixture,

the winds breathe out their last gasp,

the clouds yield no rain,

the earth be defeated of heavenly influence,

the fruits of the earth pine away as children at the withered breasts of their mother no longer able to yield them relief,

what would become of man himself, whom these things now do all serve?

See we not plainly that obedience of creatures unto the law of Nature is the stay of the whole world? Notwithstanding with Nature it cometh sometimes to pass as with art. Let Phidias [Greek sculptor] have rude and obstinate stuff to carve, though his art do that it should, his work will lack that beauty which otherwise in fitter matter it might have had. He that striketh an instrument with skill may cause notwithstanding a very unpleasant sound if the string whereon he striketh chance to be uncapable of harmony.

Exercise
Write a paragraph in imitation of Hooker's in which you build to a climax by means of a succession of related "if" clauses. The following suggestions may be of help:

1. If we should have a bad winter . . .
2. If we should lose all our money . . .
3. If there should be another world war . . .
4. If disaster should strike . . .
5. If it should turn out that I have no talent . . .

The following passage from Philip Stubbes's *The Anatomy of Abuses* is less serious than the others in this chapter and, for that matter, less "gorgeous." Its complications lie in a rapid succession of parallel structures that seem to pummel the reader the way football players pummel each other. Remember that the paragraph is presented here in a format designed to emphasize the way the sentences are structured. After you have studied it, you may wish to try your hand at writing about a family squabble, a lover's quarrel, trouble on the job, another sport, or anything threatening in a style that imitates Stubbes's.

For as concerning football playing,
  I protest unto you it may rather be called
    a friendly kind of fight,
    than a play or recreation;
    a bloody and murdering practice,
    than a fellowly sport or pastime.
  For doth not everyone lie in wait for his adversary,
    seeking to overthrow him
    and to pick [pitch] him on his nose,
    though it be upon hard stones,
    in ditch or dale,
    in valley or hill,

or what place soever it be he careth not,
   so he have him down.
And he that can serve the most of this fashion,
   he is counted the only fellow,
   and who but he?
So that by this means,
   sometimes their necks are broken,
   sometimes their backs,
   sometimes their legs,
   sometimes their arms,
   sometimes one part thrust out of joint,
   sometimes another,
   sometimes their noses gush out with blood,
   sometimes their eyes start out,
   and sometimes hurt in one place,
   sometimes in another.
But whosoever 'scapeth away the best goeth not scot-
free,
   but is either sore wounded, crazed, and bruised,
   so as he dieth of it,
   or else 'scapeth very hardly.
And no marvel, for they have the sleights
   to meet one betwixt two,
   to dash him against the heart with their elbows,
   to hit him under the short ribs with their gripped
   fists,
   and with their knees to catch him upon the hip,
   and to pick him on his neck,
   with an hundred such murdering devices.
And hereof groweth
   envy, malice, rancor, choler,
   hatred, displeasure, enmity, and what not else:
   and sometimes
   fighting, brawling, contention, quarrel-picking,
   murder, homicide, and great effusion of blood,
   as experience daily teacheth.

John Donne is our bridge to the seventeenth century, and there
are those who would place him firmly in that century's style by

virtue of the precision with which he selects his imagery and the boldness with which he directs his message to a chosen audience. "Political" as Donne's sermons may read, they owe most of their power—emotional, intellectual, spiritual, aesthetic—to his brilliant manipulation of the best elements of the Baroque Style. The nine majestic "that" clauses in the following sermon (it is one long sentence!) are thunderous organ chords that announce the verbal fugue that embellishes the clause. This is baroque writing at its grandest—brilliantly ornate, magnificently orchestrated, genuinely stirring—and yet, withal, disarmingly simple. Although the reader (or, as it was in his day, the listener) anticipates a resolution, he does not grow impatient for it; rather he fears it and almost prefers the suspense of the threat to the judgment that resolves it. Imagine a skilled orator delivering this sermon and you can begin to sense the power of Donne's prose style.

The imitation that follows is contemporary parody, guilty less of irreverence than of ineptitude. However, it may inspire you to attempt a sentence of your own in imitation of Donne's Sermon LXXVI ("On Falling out of God's Hand"):

When God's hand is bent to strike, "it is a fearful thing to fall into the hands of the living God"; but to fall out of the hands of the living God is a horror beyond our expression, beyond our imagination.

[The sentence in question begins here:]

That God should let my soul fall out of his hand into a bottomless pit and roll an unremovable stone upon it and leave it to that which it finds there (and it shall find that there which it never imagined till it came thither) and never think more of that soul, never have more to do with it;

that of that providence of God that studies the life of every weed and worm and ant and spider and toad and viper there should never, never any beam flow out upon me;

that that God who looked upon me when I was nothing and called me when I was not, as though I had been, out of the womb

and depth of darkness, will not look upon me now, when
though a miserable and a banished and a damned creature, yet
I am his creature still and contribute something to his glory
even in my damnation;

that that God who hath often looked upon me in my foulest un-
cleanness and when I had shut out the eye of the day, the sun,
and the eye of the night, the taper, and the eyes of all the
world with curtains and windows and doors, did yet see me
and see me in mercy by making me see that he saw me and
sometimes brought me to a present remorse and (for that time)
to a forbearing of that sin, should so turn himself from me to
his glorious saints and angels as that no saint nor angel nor
Christ Jesus himself should ever pray him to look towards me,
never remember him that such a soul there is;

that that God who hath so often said to my soul, *Quare morieris?*
why wilt thou die? and so often sworn to my soul, *Vivit Do-
minus,* as the Lord liveth, I would not have thee die but live,
will neither let me die nor let me live, but die an everlasting
life and live an everlasting death;

that that God who, when he could not get into me by standing
and knocking, by his ordinary means of entering, by his word,
his mercies, hath applied his judgments and hath shaked the
house, this body, with agues and palsies, and set this house
on fire with fevers and calentures [delirium], and frighted the
master of the house, my soul, with horrors and heavy appre-
hensions and so made an entrance into me;

that that God should frustrate all his own purposes and practices
upon me and leave me and cast me away as though I had cost
him nothing;

that this God at last should let this soul go away as smoke, as a
vapor, as a bubble;

and that then this soul cannot be a smoke, a vapor, nor a bubble,
but must lie in darkness as long as the Lord of light is light
itself, and never spark of that light reach to my soul;

what Tophet is not paradise,

what brimstone is not amber,

what gnashing is not a comfort,

what gnawing of the worm is not a tickling,

what torment is not a marriage bed to this damnation,
  to be secluded
  eternally, eternally eternally,
  from the sight of God?

Here is a short imitation:

When the boss's hand is bent to strike, "it is a fearful thing to
  fall into the hands of an angry boss"; but to fall out of his good
  graces is a misfortune beyond our expression, beyond belief.
That my boss should abominate my work, and refuse to look upon
  it, and attempt to disregard it, and have nothing more to do
  with it;
that that man who bestows the commonest decencies to the low-
  liest janitor and dishwasher and errand-boy should deny them
  to me;
that that generosity which he extends every Christmas to each
  and every employee, who does him service should be withheld
  from me and never again proffered;
that he who hired me and looked upon me and my work with
  favor should now behave as if I did not exist, as if I should not
  exist, as if I do not now or ever shall henceforth exist, yet I am
  still his employee and have contributed something to the company;
that that same boss who counselled me through dark days and
  comforted me in times of stress and kept faith in me when I
  had lost faith in myself and helped me to see the error of my
  ways and to overcome that error should so turn against me,
  should turn instead to others closer to him, his favored, as that
  they should never again recognize me;
that that boss who once said that I should always have my job,
  should work as long as I wanted and forever enjoy the fruits of
  my labor and the beneficence of his stewardship hath made his
  decision and shaken up my life, and caused my body to ache,
  and threatened my livelihood, and given up on me so that I
  have ceased to exist without ever again a spark of hope;
what sweat-shop is not paradise,
what long hours not sweetness,

what lowly pay not a blessing,
what abominable conditions not a marriage bed to this damnation, to be secluded
eternally, eternally, eternally,
from my boss's employment?

Exercise
Try writing a similar paragraph in which you employ a series of
extended "that" clauses. The following suggestions might help:

1. the pain of a lover's rejection
2. the agony of being excluded from the team
3. the humiliation of public disgrace (getting thrown out of class,
   into jail, off the dance floor)

The Baroque Style befitted an age of affluence and culture, an age
in which gentlemen of leisure had world enough and time to
pursue a thought through a rhetorical maze and enjoy the hunt
as much as the catch. It was an age of exuberance and exaggeration. England was on the verge of ruling the world, and the Baroque Style was a luxury the privileged allowed themselves. It
was, above all, an indulgence in sheer linguistic opulence and
shameless virtuosity that heralded the coming of age of the English language.

18. The Senecan Style

The sixteenth century was an interlude of affluence and achievement for the English. The dynamic wars of the fifteenth century had, at last, been settled, great rulers emerged to take charge of an ever more powerful nation, and the grimness of civil war was, as yet, far off. It was an age of leisure and luxury such as the English had not seen before, and its spirit is manifest in the selections you studied and imitated in the previous chapter.

As the nation gained in power, however, and as religious dissent became an increasing threat to its stability, a need arose for more forceful, less fanciful prose, for prose of a kind meant to provoke minds and, if possible, change them. What was needed was a hard-hitting "political" prose style suited to debate. Dissension and rebuttal marked the sallies between Roundheads and Cavaliers, and as the threat of civil war grew imminent and the very life of the king became endangered, the writers of the age responded with a leaner, less embroidered style.

Perhaps no other political event so altered the English language as the English Civil War of the 1640s. It was then that English assumed the shape that it has retained, with minor modifications, down to the present century. When you first read it, you may think it more complex than it really is because its sentences do remain long and, of course, its vocabulary may strike modern ears as quaint. However, examine the sentence structure and you will discover a leaning toward loose sentences, sentences made up of clauses strung together by fairly simple coordination and subordination. The periodic sentence, when it is used, is usually rather short. And parallel structure is mostly a matter of words in a series rather than elaborate phrases or clauses.

From this period on we will begin to take more notice of subject matter, for what is being said will have an increasing influence on how it is said. A grave subject calls for a sober style, while a lighter subject calls for a brighter style. Although writers at all ages have written both serious and frivolous prose, each prose period has its dominant voice. Furthermore, these periods seem to be pendular, a sober style eminent in one period, a lighter style eminent in the next. Thus, there is a rough parallel between the more "artful" prose of the sixteenth, eighteenth, and twentieth centuries and between the more "skillful" prose of the seventeenth and nineteenth centuries. "Artful" prose is prose that emphasizes form over content. "Skillful" prose is prose that emphasizes content over form.

Thomas Hobbes was certainly one of the most serious men of the seventeenth century. He was extremely pessimistic about the nature of man and extremely conservative about the nature of government. His greatest work, *The Leviathan,* is a very important and very serious treatise on government. Here is one sentence from it.

A commonwealth is said to be instituted
   when a multitude of men do agree and covenant,
   everyone one with every one,
   that to whatsoever man, or assembly of men
   shall be given by the major part
   the right to present the person of them all
   (that is to say, to be their representative);
   every one,
   as well he that voted for it

as he that voted against it,
shall authorize all the actions and judgments of that man,
or assembly of men,
in the same manner as if they were his own,
to the end to live peaceably amongst themselves
and be protected against other men.

Today we might put it this way:

A commonwealth exists when a body of men authorize an
elected representative to act on their behalf to secure their peace
and protection.

This may be the gist of Hobbes's sentence, but it lacks the com-
prehensiveness and precision of his statement, which has almost
a legal tone to it. It is a complete definition; and, if you study it
carefully, you will discover that the main idea continues straight-
forwardly and clearly through the sentence. It is the sentence's
interruptions, not its convolutions, that make modern readers
blink and go back. Here is an imitation of Hobbes's sentence:

A family is said to be happy
when all the members do agree and covenant,
every one with every one,
that to whatsoever member, or members,
shall be given by the others
a duty to perform
(that is to say, a responsibility)
every one,
as well he that approved of it
as he that did not,
shall respect the rights of that member,
or members,
in the same manner as if they were his own,
to the end to live peaceably amongst themselves
and be free from envy and conceit.

Exercise

Choose one of the following suggestions and construct a Hobbes-
ian sentence of your own:

1. A classroom is said to be productive when . . .
2. An office is said to be efficient when . . .
3. A party is said to be successful when . . .
4. A club meeting is said to be running smoothly when . . .
5. A team is said to be playing well when . . .

John Milton, the towering presence of the seventeenth century, was an irascible old Puritan who, like most zealots, was capable of staggering logic when his cause was most self-serving. He was thoroughly involved in the Commonwealth government of Oliver Cromwell and thoroughly disillusioned when that paradise was lost. As Cromwell's Latin Secretary, Milton contended with the best minds in Europe—and usually won, won the battle at least, if not the war. Much of what he wrote is almost unreadable today because, among other things, we find the matter meaningless and the style therefore tedious. On the subjects of divorce or censorship, however, matters dear to Milton's heart, he wrote lucidly and brilliantly. The treatise on censorship, *Aeropagitica*, makes one wonder whether Milton was not a more nimble politician than a poet, when one stops to think of how the Puritans closed down the theatres and spread repression throughout the land. Nevertheless, it stands yet today as the last word on the subject, and it is from this treatise that the following two paragraphs have been excerpted. You can feel the touch of the poet in the magnificent prose.

As therefore the state of man now is,
    what wisdom can there be to choose,
    what continence to forbear
    without the knowledge of evil?
He that can apprehend and consider vice
    with all her baits
    and seeming pleasures,
    and yet abstain,
    and yet distinguish,
    and yet prefer that

which is truly better,
he is the true wayfaring Christian.
I cannot praise a fugitive and cloistered virtue,
unexercised and unbreathed,
that never sallies out and sees her adversary,
but slinks out of the race
where that immortal garland is to be run for,
not without dust and heat.
Assuredly we bring not innocence into the world,
we bring impurity much rather;
that which purifies us is trial,
and trial is by what is contrary.
That virtue, therefore, which is but a youngling
in the contemplation of evil,
and knows not the utmost
that vice promises to her followers,
and rejects it,
is but a blank virtue,
not a pure;
her whiteness is but an excremental whiteness;

. . .

Since therefore the knowledge and survey of vice
is in this world so necessary
to the constituting of human virtue,
and the scanning of error
to the confirmation of truth,
how can we more safely,
and with less danger,
scout into the regions of sin and falsity
than by reading all manner of tractates
and hearing all manner of reason?
And this is the benefit
which may be had of books
promiscuously read.

Analyze Milton's sentence structure. Notice how his use of *peri-odic* and *balanced* sentences is so skillful that the point is sharp-ened, not obscured, by rhetoric. His is a clean, relatively straightforward style even though it is ornamented with parallelism and antithesis and figurative language.

The second to the last sentence in the Milton excerpt is written in the form of a question. Rhetorical questions, as these are called, are largely out of fashion today. They are frowned upon as evasions of the issue: the writer's job is to answer questions, not ask them. In the seventeenth century, however, the rhetorical question was used frequently and with great effectiveness. Daniel Defoe, a writer whose temper inclines him more toward the eighteenth century (into which he lived) than the seventeenth, is a transitional prose stylist whose subject matter anticipates the happier concerns of the Augustans while it still retains the thrust and parry of the seventeenth-century verbal fencers.

The fall of the Commonwealth and the restoration of the king spelled an end to the need for Senecan sobriety and ushered in an age of welcome levity. The following excerpt from Defoe's "An Academy for Women" makes an excellent bridge between the prose styles of the seventeenth and eighteenth centuries because its subject matter is serious, but not too serious, and its style is light, but not too light. Notice the generous use of the rhetorical question.

The soul is placed in the body like a rough diamond,
    and must be polished,
    or the lustre of it will never appear:
    and 'tis manifest that
    as the rational soul distinguishes us from brutes,
    so education carries on the distinction
    and makes some less brutish than others.
This is too evident to need any demonstration.
But why then should women be denied the benefit of instruction?
If knowledge and understanding had been useless additions to
    the sex,
    God Almighty would never have given them capacities,
    for he made nothing needless.

Besides, I would ask such what they can see in ignorance
    that they should think it a necessary ornament to a woman?
    or how much worse is a wise woman than a fool?
    or what has the woman done to forfeit the privilege
    of being taught?
Does she plague us with her pride and impertinence?
Why did we not let her learn,
    that she might have had more wit?
Shall we upbraid women with folly,
    when 'tis only the error of this inhuman custom
    that hindered them being made wiser?

Exercise

Write a paragraph in imitation of Defoe's in which you argue for
some form of equality. Use rhetorical questions. The following
suggestions may be helpful.

1. equal job opportunities for women (minorities)
2. equal pay for women (minorities)

Here is another paragraph by Defoe from the same treatise, one
that might be easier to imitate. Notice the use of parallelism, particularly the words in a series that are usually triads. This will
become a favorite eighteenth-century stylistic trait.

If her temper be good,
    want of education makes her soft and easy.
Her wit,
        for want of teaching,
    makes her impertinent and talkative.
Her knowledge,
        for want of judgment and experience,
    makes her fanciful and whimsical.
If her temper be bad,
    want of breeding makes her worse;
    and she grows haughty, insolent, and loud.
If she be passionate,
    want of manners makes her a termagant and a scold,

which is much at one with lunatic.
If she be proud,
  want of discretion (which still is breeding)
  makes her conceited, fantastic, and ridiculous.
And from these she degenerates to be turbulent, clamorous,
  noisy, nasty, and the devil.

Here is a paragraph written in imitation of this latter one of Defoe's:

If her looks be good,
  lack of polish makes her even more attractive.
Her ignorance, for lack of learning,
  makes her cute and appealing.
Her behavior, for lack of judgment and experience,
  makes her impulsive and outgoing.
If her looks be bad,
  her lack of training makes her worse;
  and she grows sullen, self-pitying, and mean.
If she be passionate,
  lack of looks makes her aggressive and bold,
  which is much at one with a hooker.
If she be proud,
  lack of looks makes her arrogant, cynical, and sly.
And from these she degenerates to be resentful, vindictive,
  spiteful, intolerant, gross, and a witch.

Exercise
Try to fill out the following paragraph in a manner imitative of Defoe:

If his digestion be good,

_____

His appetite,

_____

His weight,

_____

If his digestion be bad,

_____

If he be in charge,

_____

If he be married,

_____

And from these he degenerates to be _____

_____

Few writers since the time of Milton have quite been able to maintain that delicate balance between gravity of tone and elegance of presentation that characterizes the Senecan Style. The Augustans were more often subtle than solemn, the Victorians more often solemn than subtle. In modern times, a fair facsimile of the Senecan Style enjoyed its finest hour in the stirring speeches of Winston Churchill during World War II, and its stamp can be found on every page of his monumental history of that war. The disciples of Seneca may not always be in fashion, but they are never out of style.

19. The Augustan Style

The court of Charles II saw the restored king as a new Caesar Augustus ushering in an age of taste, elegance, and wit. These self-styled "Augustans" set a tone and pace in life and art that were to dominate every aspect of the culture for nearly a century and a half. Between the English Civil War and the French Revolution, English culture reached its most civilized heights. The key words were "elegance," "refinement," "decorum," "reasonableness," "sensibility." Each of these elements found its way into the distinctive prose style of the period.

It would be unfair to say that the Augustans were not concerned with profound matters, but it would be more honest to say that they were more inclined to take light things seriously and serious things lightly. They preferred minuets to metaphysics, mirth to melancholy, wit to wisdom (though they would have argued that wit and wisdom are one and the same). They cared more about their manners than about their souls; their concerns were less holy than wholly secular. They had a high opinion of themselves and the high spirits to carry it off with style. They worshiped balance and restraint, disdained excess, and ended up refining themselves out of existence.

Before they departed, however, they left an indelible and endearing mark on our cultural heritage. Among so many other contributions, their prose style, all too frequently misunderstood today, has remained for the connoisseur of the art of language a model of sanity and sophistication. It was developed on the assumption that all men are created rational and are endowed by their creator with the faculties of right reason, moral sensibility, and mutual respect. Behold the Declaration of Independence and the United States Constitution! Both are models of brevity and of the kind of clarity that presumes a clear intelligence on the part of the reader, an intelligence that would be insulted by explanation and hair-splitting.

Although the men (and women) of the eighteenth century were actively engaged in public affairs, politics as a grim preoccupation does not return to the center stage of prose writing until the time of the American and French revolutions. Meanwhile, the topics of the day were, as you will see, things like "punning," "clothes," "friendship," "critics," "idleness," "patronage," "gentlemanly behavior," and "aesthetics." See if you think the style matches the content. Observe, as you read, how given the Augustans were to coordination, subordination, and triadic parallelism. Together they give their sentences the similarity that makes the Augustan style immediately recognizable.

Here is a selection written early in the eighteenth century. The author is the renowned essayist, Joseph Addison, who, together with Richard Steele, contributed enormously to the Augustan Style. This selection is from their journal, *The Spectator*, issue No. 61.

There is no kind of false wit
  which has been so recommended
    by the practice of all ages
  as that which consists
    in a jingle of words,
    and is comprehended
      under the general name of punning.
It is indeed impossible to kill a weed
  which the soil has a natural disposition to produce.

The seeds of punning are in the minds of all men,
  and though they may be subdued by
    reason,
    reflection,
    and good sense,
  they will be very apt to shoot up
    in the greatest genius
      that is not broken and cultivated
        by the rules of art.
Imitation is natural to us.
  and when it does not raise the mind to
    poetry,
    painting,
    music
    or other more noble arts,
  it often breaks out
    in puns and quibbles.

Here is a short passage from Jane Austen's *Northanger Abbey*, a parody of the Gothic novel, written in 1797–98 but not published until 1818. Notice not only the use of parallelism but particularly her subtle manipulation of prepositional phrases.

It would be mortifying to the feelings of many ladies,
  could they be made to understand
  how little the heart of man is affected
    by what is costly or new in their attire;
  how little it is biassed
    by the texture of their muslin,
  and how unsusceptible of peculiar tenderness
    towards the spotted,
      the sprigged,
      the mull, or
      the jaconet.
Woman is fine for her own satisfaction alone.
No man will admire her the more,
no woman will like her the better
  for it.

Neatness and fashion are enough
  for the former,
and a something of shabbiness or impropriety
will be most endearing
  to the latter.

Here is the "inimitable" Samuel Johnson (whom you are going to be asked to imitate anyway!) in an excerpt from his periodical, *The Idler* (No. 60).

Criticism is a study
  by which men grow important and formidable
    at a very small expense.
The power of invention has been conferred by nature upon few,
and the labour of learning those sciences
  which may by mere labour be obtained
is too great to be willingly endured;
but every man can exert
  such judgment as he has
    upon the works of others;
and he whom nature has made weak,
  and idleness keeps ignorant,
may yet support his vanity
  by the name of critic.

Samuel Johnson *is* the eighteenth century, and it is easy to see why, even from this fragment. His temperament was so suited to his topic, and his style to both, that he manages the perfect blend. He demolishes with deadly accuracy a favorite adversary and thoroughly enjoys every minute of it.

We shy away from satire today, or at least from personal attacks in public. We are painfully aware of one another's rights and fear that ridiculing someone (no matter how much it may be deserved) will land us in court or court public disfavor. For this reason, our humor is largely directed at ourselves. Our comedians and humorists cast only velvet-tipped barbs at other people and save their cheapest shots for themselves. The Augustans had no such scruples, and indeed would have considered them dishonest. They dipped their barbs in venom (or "spleen" as they would have said) and delighted fully as much in receiving as in giving pain. To them, insult, like imitation, was high flattery indeed.

Here is Samuel Johnson in a sober, moralizing mood. He loved to pontificate. After all, posturing is the bedfellow of wit. This paragraph is presented in a form intended to emphasize its structure.

But Idleness predominates in many lives
   where it is not suspected;
   for being a vice which terminates in itself,
   it may be enjoyed without injury to others;
   and is therefore not watched like Fraud,
   which endangers property,
   or like Pride,
   which naturally seeks its gratifications
   in another's inferiority.
Idleness is a silent and peaceful quality,
   that neither raises envy by ostentation,
   nor hatred by opposition;
   and therefore nobody is busy
   to censure or detect it.

Exercise

Fill out the following paragraph in imitation of Johnson's:

But procrastination _____
   where _____
   for _____
   it may _____
   and is _____
   which _____
   or like _____
   which _____
   in _____
Procrastination is _____
   that _____
   nor _____

and _____

to _____

If Johnson is the eighteenth-century savant, Lord Chesterfield is
the embodiment of the eighteenth-century smoothie. Johnson was
its mind, Chesterfield its manners. Each was everything the other
was not; Chesterfield was surface, Johnson substance. Perhaps
each envied the other; it's hard to say. Certainly each had a
grudging admiration for the other. That is why Johnson, in the
famous letter rejecting Chesterfield's patronage, is so bitter. The
pain shows through.

The circumstance surrounding the letter is this: all the while
Johnson was working on his monumental dictionary, he sought
Lord Chesterfield's patronage. When, upon completion of the
project, Johnson was offered this patronage, he felt insulted, this
time without feeling flattered. Here is an excerpt, presented so
as to demonstrate its style:

Is not a patron, my Lord,
   one who looks with unconcern
   on a man struggling for life in the water,
   and, when he has reached ground,
   encumbers him with help?
The notice which you have been pleased to take of my labors,
   had it been early, had been kind;
   but it has been delayed
   till I am indifferent, and cannot enjoy it;
   till I am solitary, and cannot impart it;
   till I am known, and do not want it.
I hope it is no very cynical asperity
   not to confess obligations
   where no benefit has been received,
   or to be unwilling
   that the public should consider me
   as owing that to a patron
   which Providence has enabled me
   to do for myself.

Here is an imitation (with all due respect) of this excerpt from Johnson's letter to Lord Chesterfield:

Is not an employer, sir,
   one who looks with unconcern
   on a worker struggling to meet a quota,
   and, when he has just about made it,
   asks him if he needs any help?
The notice which you have been pleased to take of my labors,
   had it been some time ago, had been appreciated;
   but it has been held back
   till I am tired, and cannot believe it;
   till I am independent, and cannot accept it;
   till I am mad, and do not want it.
I hope it is not sheer ingratitude
   not to recognize assistance
   where none has been forthcoming,
   or to be upset
   that people should think
   I owe to an employer
   what I have been able, with God's help,
   to do by myself.

Exercise
Write a similar imitation of Johnson's letter, addressing yours to a professor.

Lord Chesterfield himself was no slouch when it came to writing letters. His letters of advice to his son are models of urbanity and sophistication, his concerns typical of the superficial concerns of the day. The advice is essentially practical and only accidentally moral. In this respect, Chesterfield reflects the "virtue rewarded" syndrome of the century. Whether you behaved or misbehaved did not matter so long as you acted with prudence. It was imprudent to get caught—or to catch anything. It was smart to do the proper (not to be confused with "right") thing. It will take the Victorians to put the stuffing back into "proper."

Lord Chesterfield is not the greatest stylist of the age, but there is a charm and gentlemanly grace about his prose that is representative of the best of the minor writers. Here is an excerpt from Letter CXLII:

Every excellency and every virtue
  has its kindred vice or weakness,
  and, if carried beyond certain bounds,
  sinks into one or the other.
Generosity often runs into profusion,
  economy into avarice,
  courage into rashness,
  caution into timidity,
  and so on:—
  insomuch that, I believe,
  there is more judgment required
  for the proper conduct of our virtues
  than for avoiding their opposite vices.
Vice in its true light is so deformed
  that it shocks us at first sight,
  and would hardly ever seduce us,
  if it did not at first wear the mask of some virtue.
But virtue is in itself so beautiful
  that it charms us at first sight;
  engages us more and more upon further acquaintance;
  and, as with other beauties,
  we think excess is impossible:
  it is here that judgment is necessary
  to moderate and direct the effects
  of an excellent cause.
I shall apply this reasoning, at present,
  not to any particular virtue,
  but to an excellency,
  which for want of judgment is often the cause
  of ridiculous and blamable effects;
  I mean, great learning,
  which, if not accompanied with sound judgment,

frequently carries us
into error, pride, and pedantry.

Alexander Pope counseled us that "a little learning is a danger-
ous thing." Now we have an aristocrat warning his son, who is
away at college, about the perils of too much learning.

Exercise
Try your hand at imitating Lord Chesterfield's style, using one of
the following openings.

1. Every advantage has its disadvantage
2. Every reward has its punishment
3. Every favor has its obligation
4. Every achievement has its price
5. Every pleasure has its pain

Here is the great painter of the eighteenth century, Sir Joshua
Reynolds, discoursing before the Royal Academy on the value of
imitation:

When we have had continually before us the great works of art
to impregnate our minds with kindred ideas, we are then, and
not till then, fit to produce something of the same species. We
behold all about us with the eyes of those penetrating observers
whose works we contemplate; and our minds, accustomed to
think the thoughts of the noblest and brightest intellects, are prepared for the discovery and selection of all that is great and noble
in nature. The greatest natural genius cannot subsist on its own
stock; he who resolves never to ransack any mind but his own
will be soon reduced, from mere barrenness, to the poorest of all
imitations; he will be obliged to imitate himself, and to repeat
what he has before often repeated. When we know the subject
designed by such men, it will never be difficult to guess what
kind of work is to be produced.

That wonderful word "ransack" is one of the earliest indications
of a breakthrough, a loosening up (in the eighteenth of all cen-

turies!) of the rules of diction, a foreshadowing of the exciting linguistic freedom of modern times. There is still a long way to go (the Victorians loom ominously ahead), but language will have its own way with its own words.

The eighteenth century went out with a bang, and amid turmoil and revolution and an emerging romantic spirit full of high purpose and intensity, the English language was mustered into the service of Great Causes. There was a new gravity in its tone and more backbone in its style. Here is an example of this "elegance in uniform" from *Reflections on the Revolution in France* by Edmund Burke, a closet conservative in his youth who "came out" after the horrors of the Reign of Terror. Burke continues to be the guru of conservativism. This excerpt may give you a hint as to why. See how Burke marshals the Augustan Style and makes it march to a different drummer.

They [revolutionaries] see no merit
  in the good,
and no fault
  in the vicious,
    management of public affairs;
they rather rejoice in the latter,
  as more propitious to revolution.
They see no merit or demerit
  in any man,
  or any action,
  or any political principle,
    any further than as they may forward or retard
      their design of change:
they therefore take up,
  one day
    the most violent and stretched prerogative,
and another time
    the wildest democratic ideas of freedom,
and pass from one to the other
  without any sort of regard
    to cause,

> to person,
> or to party.

There is a curious contradiction peculiar to the Augustan Style. On the one hand it is so polished, so lucid, and so charming that it would seem to have set a model for fine prose ever after: for who could improve on it? On the other hand, it is so much a product and reflection of its times that any attempt to use it since has suffered by sounding painfully anachronistic. Like two or three measures of Mozart, two or three phrases from this style relate it instantly and irrefutably to its cultural era. As with everything else good about the eighteenth century, it was too good to last. It is more fun than any other style to imitate, however, and aside from what it may do for (or to) your own style, it's a good style to keep in reserve in case the world ever comes to its senses again.

20. The Victorian Style

The graceful world of the Augustans was too delicately balanced to survive the two revolutions that converged upon it as the eighteenth century died: the Industrial Revolution and the French Revolution. Together these revolutions shifted power to the middle classes and completely reorganized society. Separately they established contradictory forces which, in turn, created tensions that were to polarize moral judgment. On the one hand, science was destroying many of man's cherished illusions and technology was threatening to enslave him; on the other hand, democratic rule encouraged man to think better of himself, to trust himself to handle his own affairs, to dream of redemption through political freedom.

The tension between these poles was fierce. The Romantics, who dominated the early decades of the nineteenth century, met the challenge head on. They found the climate exciting, inspiring, invigorating. They fled the cities for the mountaintops, shook their fists at Heaven, and declared man exalted and invincible. They were mostly solitary rebels who refused to be taken in by either science or politics. Hard on the heels of their idealism came the Victorian pragmatists, eager to compromise, eager to get ahead. For rebellion they substituted zeal and set about tidying up the moral disorder with a vengeance.

All of life needed re-examining and reconfiguring, and these eminent Victorians stoically accepted the burden of discovering the true nature of man, of determining what his purpose was, and of deciding how he was to behave. They began by assuming that man's primary obligation was to Duty. Duty demanded unswerving loyalty and unflagging faith. One's duty was what one did; there was no question about it. To know what one's duty was and to carry it out without complaint was a test of character. It is easy to see why the word "duty" soon came to connote something unpleasant. In fact, the more unpleasant one's duty, the stronger one's moral fiber in carrying it out. There was a job to be done, and it was no laughing matter. How could there be time for whimsy and frivolity when there was a world out there to guide and educate?

Duty, then, became a religion, and the zeal with which it was performed amounted to a breed of evangelicalism that gives much Victorian prose its quality of earnestness. Once you have studied and imitated some of these zealous Victorians, you will not wonder why a weary Oscar Wilde, at the end of the century, was questioning the importance of being earnest.

Meanwhile, American literature had come of age, and although American writers were busy examining themselves and the world about them with Romantic intensity, they were rendering their findings in a style not unlike that of the leading English essayists of the time.

Here is Henry David Thoreau, writing from Walden Pond, expressing a major concern of the nineteenth century: individualism. In this opening paragraph from "Where I Lived, and What I Lived For," pay particular attention to the succession of infinitive phrases.

I went to the woods because I wished
   to live deliberately,
   to front only the essential facts of life,
   and see if I could not learn what it had to teach,
   and not

    when I came to die,
      discover that I had not lived.
I did not wish
  to live what was not life,
    living is so dear;
nor did I wish
  to practice resignation,
    unless it was quite necessary.
I wanted
  to live deep
  and suck out all the marrow of life,
  to live so sturdily and Spartan-like as
  to put to rout all that was not life,
  to cut a broad swath and shave close,
  to drive life into a corner,
    and reduce it to its lowest terms,
and, if it proved to be mean, why then
  to get the whole and genuine meanness of it,
  and publish its meanness to the world;
or if it were sublime,
  to know it by experience,
  and be able
  to give a true account of it
    in my next excursion.

Here is an imitation of the third sentence from the above paragraph:

I wanted
  to work hard
  and get everything I could out of the experience,
  to throw so much into it as
  to leave no time for fear,
  to take my aim and aim high,
  to push my abilities to the limit,
    and find out what I could do,
and, if I failed, why then
  to get to the bottom of that failure,
  and broadcast it to the world;

or if I were successful,
   to understand what it takes,
   and be able
   to explain its mystery
     to those who would succeed me.

Exercise

Write a similar sentence in imitation of Thoreau. Use either one of the following suggestions or an idea of your own.

1. I wanted to exercise well . . .
2. I wanted to perform well . . .

Emerson has a unique prose style—and one that is not necessarily worthwhile to imitate. He is famous for his islands of brilliance in a sea of obscurity. The following paragraph is fairly straightforward. It is included here mostly to illustrate the gravity with which the concept of individualism affected the men of the age.

What I must do is all that concerns me, not what the people think. This rule, equally arduous in actual and in intellectual life, may serve for the whole distinction between greatness and meanness. It is the harder, because you will always find those who think they know what is your duty better than you know it. It is easy in the world to live after the world's opinion; it is easy in solitude to live after our own; but the great man is he who in the midst of the crowd keeps with perfect sweetness the independence of solitude.

This excerpt is from Emerson's essay "Self-Reliance." Other parts of it are even more stirring. Sentences and phrases like "Trust thyself: every heart vibrates to that iron string," and "we are . . . guides, redeemers, and benefactors, . . . advancing on Chaos and the Dark" will tell you that Emerson meant business. Notice the call to Duty in the passage above and how it is associated with words like "arduous" and "harder." Notice also how the true individual becomes a "great man."

Here is a passage on the same subject by John Stuart Mill, an English contemporary of Emerson's. Notice the sobriety of this delivery. Notice also the early fear of automation and the insistence on the idea of man as a tree—organic, unique, a thing (maybe a law) unto himself. Only the sentences to be imitated are presented in an altered format.

He who lets the world,
  or his own portion of it,
  choose his plan of life for him,
  has no need of any other faculty
  than the ape-like one of imitation.
He who chooses his plan for himself,
    employs all his faculties.
He must use
  observation to see,
  reasoning and judgement to foresee,
  activity to gather materials for decision,
  discrimination to decide,
    and when he has decided,
  firmness and self-control
    to hold to his deliberate decision.
And these qualities he requires and exercises exactly in proportion as the part of his conduct which he determines according to his own judgement and feelings is a large one. It is possible that he might be guided in some good path, and kept out of harm's way, without any of these things. But what will be his comparative worth as a human being? It really is of importance, not only what men do, but also what manner of men they are that do it. Among the works of man, which human life is rightly employed in perfecting and beautifying, the first in importance surely is man himself. Supposing it were possible to get houses built, corn grown, battles fought, causes tried, and even churches erected and prayers said, by machinery—by automatons in human form— it would be a considerable loss to exchange for these automatons even the men and women who at present inhabit the more civilized parts of the world, and who assuredly are but starved specimens of what nature can and will produce. Human nature is not

a machine to be built after a model, and set to do exactly the work prescribed for it, but a tree, which requires to grow and develop itself on all sides, according to the tendency of the inward forces which make it a living thing.

An interesting thing about Mill and many Victorians is the way they make subjective pronouncements sound as if they are self-evident truths. When Mill says, "Among the works of man . . . the first in importance surely is man himself," just saying it does not make it so. Yet the statement has what we like to call "the ring of truth." The only truth apparent here is the one that says: the more unimportant man has been proved to be, the more importance he has attached to himself. It is always true of writers, but perhaps truer of Victorian writers, that the impact of their arguments has less to do with logic than with the readers' willingness to believe.

Here is an imitation of the first three sentences of the paragraph from Mill's "Of Individuality."

He who lets smoking,
  or any bad habit,
  dictate his life for him,
  has no need of any other faculty
  than the ape-like one of conditioned reflex.
He who decides to break a bad habit,
  employs all his faculties.
He must use
  determination to make the break,
  will power to persevere,
  foresight to anticipate hardships,
  incentive to succeed,
    and when he has succeeded,
  firmness and self-control
    not to backslide.

Exercise

Write three sentences in similar imitation of Mill's style using one of the following suggestions or an idea of your own:

1. He who lets other people do his work for him . . .
2. He who refuses to see both sides of a question . . .

Matthew Arnold was one of the finest prose stylists of the Victorian period—and one of the most concerned individuals who ever lived. Arnold worried about culture, about science, about education, about the quality of life. In his prose you can sense in his sincerity and his honest fear that he is almost single-handedly protecting civilization against the onslaught of the "Philistines" (his term for the crude and vulgar). Arnold was also a fine poet, and it is the poet's finer ear that infuses the following paragraph, from "Preface to Poems," with harmony.

The confusion of the present times is great,
the multitude of voices counseling different things bewildering,
the number of existing works capable of attracting a young writ-
     er's attention and of becoming his models, immense.
What he wants is a hand to guide him through the confusion,
a voice to prescribe to him the aim which he should keep in
     view,
and to explain to him that the value of the literary works which
     offer themselves to his attention
is relative to their power of helping him forward on his road
     towards this aim.
Such a guide
     the English writer at the present day will nowhere find.
Failing this,
     all that can be looked for,
     all indeed that can be desired is,
that his attention should be fixed on excellent models;
that he may reproduce,
     at any rate,
          something of their excellence,
               by penetrating himself with their works and
               by catching their spirit,
if he cannot be taught
     to produce what is excellent independently.

Here is an imitation of Arnold's grand opening sentence:

The atmosphere of the present times is tense,
the variety of prophets preaching contradictory things unsettling,
the number of living statesmen capable of firing a young person's
    enthusiasm and of becoming his heroes, negligible.
Here is another:
The attitude of the present times is negative,
the abundance of gloom-mongers predicting imminent doom
    disquieting,
the threat of existing arsenals capable of unparalleled devastation
    and perhaps global annihilation, enormous.

Exercise
Write a sentence about the present times in a style that imitates
Arnold's.

It is not a well enough known fact that Charles Darwin was a fine
prose stylist as well as a fine naturalist. His *On the Origin of Species* remains a classic work of literature as much as of science.
Here is a paragraph from a later work, *The Descent of Man,* a title
as often misunderstood as his findings. Actually, he never worried about the ramifications of his findings. He left that to others.
Darwin was the consummate scientist who respected facts and
disdained idle speculation. The irony is that he went about his
duty with the high-mindedness of the best of the Victorians,
seemingly oblivious to the fact that his evolutionary theories
would become revolutionary concepts destined to undermine
duty, zeal, earnestness, and all the rest of the sacred Victorian
virtues. Notice the delicacy with which he comes to his stunning
conclusion. Only the final sentence is presented in an altered format.

Man may be excused for feeling some pride at having risen,
though not through his own exertions, to the very summit of the
organic scale; and the fact of his having thus risen, instead of
having been aboriginally placed there, may give him hopes for a

still higher destiny in the distant future. But we are not here
concerned with hopes or fears, only with the truth as far as our
reason allows us to discover it.
I have given the evidence to the best of my ability;
   and we must acknowledge,
   as it seems to me, that man
     with all his noble qualities
     with sympathy which feels for the most debased,
     with benevolence which extends not only to other men
       but to the humblest living creature,
     with his godlike intellect
       which has penetrated into the movements
       and constitution of the solar system—
Man still bears in his bodily frame
    the indelible stamp of his lowly origins.

It was the popularizers of Darwin's theories, men like Thomas
Henry Huxley, who beat people over the head with the monkey
business and got them all riled up. As you see, Darwin is almost
apologetic about the conclusions he draws. He is self-effacing
about his own judgment and quick to smooth man's feathers before he plucks them. Put this way, it makes one wonder what all
the fuss was (or is) about.

Here is an imitation of the last sentence of the Darwin paragraph, beginning just after the semicolon:

. . . and we must acknowledge,
   as it seems to me, that professors
   with all their good qualities,
   with training of the most thorough kind,
   with experience at many levels and in many areas,
   with their scholarship
     which has advanced their own learning
     and that of others in their fields—
   with all these excellent qualities—
Professors must still remember that their students
   come first.

Exercise

Write a similar sentence in imitation of Darwin's, using either one of the following suggestions or an idea of your own:

1. women
2. students
3. robots

It is interesting to note that some of the finest writers of the Victorian age were not prose stylists by profession but economists (Mill) or scientists (Darwin) or theologians (Newman) who happened to write well. In fact, they were likely to write better than professed men of letters like Hazlitt or Ruskin or Pater. Differences in skill aside, they all shared that sense of mission that distinguishes the Victorian Style. What it lacked in snap and sparkle, it made up for in high moral purpose. The wonder is that it worked as well as it did. The trick seems to be in the quality of the conviction with which so much Victorian prose was written. You can't fake faith, and there is little that is phony about what the best of them had to say regardless of how untenable their positions may seem to us today. The sparkle may be missing, but there was no skimping on starch.

21. The Modern Style

If there is one thing that distinguishes the Modern Style from earlier prose styles, it is that it seems so effortless. We know, however, from twentieth-century writers like Maugham and Orwell just how much effort actually went into such effortlessness. On this side of the Atlantic, and at about the same time, H. L. Mencken was honing his own effortless style and promoting stylistic innovation both in what he said and how he said it.

Here he is, in a passage from *The American Language,* practicing what he preaches as he launches yet another attack against his favorite target, the "booboisie." Notice that within rather traditional sentence structure, he relaxes the rules of diction to give the Modern Style its unmistakably "fresh" American ring.

The American is not, of course, lacking in a capacity for discipline;
   he has it highly developed;
   he submits to leadership readily,
   and even to tyranny.
But, by a curious twist, it is not the leadership that is old and decorous that commonly fetches him, but the leadership that is new and extravagant. He will resist dictation out of the past, but

he will follow a new messiah with almost Russian willingness, and into the wildest vagaries of economics, religion, morals and speech.
A new fallacy in politics spreads faster in the United States
     than anywhere else on earth,
  and so does a new fashion in hats,
  or a new revelation of God,
  or a new means of killing time,
  or a new shibboleth,
  or metaphor,
  or piece of slang.
Thus the American, on his linguistic side, likes to make his language as he goes along, and not all the hard work of the school-marm can hold the business back.

There is satire here bordering on cynicism. It is a note that will be sounded again and again in twentieth-century writing. Darwin, Marx, and Freud did their work well, and the children of the new century were not to be caught in unguarded moments of sentimentality or evangelicalism. Things bothered them all right; everything bothered them. One by one their gods had been demolished and there seemed only charlatans arising to take their place. You could trust nothing and no one, not even yourself. It's not without reason that this century has been termed "the age of anxiety."

Anxiety, as we have come to learn, is often released in morbid, nervous laughter. This may explain why there is a humorous strain running through even the dourest of twentieth-century writing, as if the cardinal sin is to take anything seriously, to do anything but giggle as the *Titanic* sinks. Thus, caught as we are between self-deprecation and self-exaltation, we have developed a style of self-criticism that tries to satirize our foibles and, at the same time, mock the satirist.

Catch the self-mocking tone in Mencken's criticism of American culture, as if to say that he means what he says but that he knows he's a fool for saying it. Again, parts of the paragraph have been rearranged to demonstrate the author's debt to an earlier prose style.

The capital defect in the culture of These States
    is the lack of a civilized aristocracy,
  secure in its position,
  animated by an intelligent curiosity,
  skeptical of all facile generations,
  superior to the sentimentality of the mob,
  and delighting in the battle of ideas for its own sake.
The word I use, despite the qualifying adjective, has got itself meanings, of course, that I by no means intend to convey. Any mention of an aristocracy, to a public fed upon democratic fustian, is bound to bring up images
    of stockbrokers' wives lolling obscenely in opera boxes,
    or of haughty Englishmen slaughtering whole generations of
       grouse in an inordinate and incomprehensible manner,
    or of bogus counts coming over to work their magic upon the
       daughters of breakfast-food and bathtub kings.
This misconception belongs to the general American tradition.

Here is an imitation of the first sentence of the above paragraph:

A capital defect in the modern family
    is the lack of a central authority,
  strong in principle,
  motivated by a desire for justice,
  suspicious of self-preserving interests,
  above partiality and discrimination,
  and delighting in the unity of the family
     for its own sake.

Exercise

Write a sentence of your own in imitation of Mencken's. Use either one of the following suggestions or an idea of your own.

1. A capital defect in the university . . .
2. A capital defect in the government . . .

If one had to pick out the major preoccupation of Americans, and of American writers, in this century it would probably be the continuing and overriding concern with self. The abstract Man as the center of the universe has become particular men (and now women) as centers of their own private worlds. Modern prose is strewn with the jargon of self: identity, alienation, me first, *numero uno,* pulling your own strings, I am my own best friend, looking out for number one, I'm O.K., you're O.K. (or not O.K.). The modern brand of self-centeredness, however, has not produced the Augustan snob, the Romantic egoist, or the Victorian prophet who could lacerate his brethren's follies without batting an eye. Modern man may swagger and boast, but it is mostly a pose. Underneath he is insecure and morbidly afraid of humiliation. For this reason, he finds satire uncomfortable and refuses to indulge in it for fear the tables will be turned and he will become the target. Recently, there have been healthy signs of the return of social satire, mostly in the form of lampooning, which is usually exaggerated enough or gross enough either to amuse its victims or miss them entirely. Meanwhile, the only socially acceptable form of satire is self-satire, the mainstay of stand-up comedians.

To be the butt of one's own jokes is a form of purgation through public exposure. It's a rich and rewarding lode to mine if mined within reason, but when it turns into verbal self-flagellation, it can become psychotic.

James Thurber wrote wittily and charmingly about his own shortcomings, but he always managed to do so with taste and restraint. The following passage, though not specifically about himself, is representative of the we're-all-in-the-same-boat brand of satire that simply chastizes the collective rather than the individual self. As you read it, notice that Thurber is one man speaking, from painful experience, about all men.

The male fiddler crab has a somewhat easier time, but it can hardly be said that he is sitting pretty. He has one enormously large and powerful claw, usually brilliantly colored, and you might suppose that all he had to do was reach out and grab some passing cutie. The very earliest fiddler crabs may have tried this, but, if so, they got slapped for their pains. A female fiddler crab will not tolerate any caveman stuff; she never has and she doesn't intend to start now. To attract a female, a fiddler crab has to stand on tiptoe and brandish his claw in the air. If any female in the neighborhood is interested—and you'd be surprised how many are not—she comes over and engages him in light badinage, for which he is not in the mood. As many as a hundred females may pass the time of day with him and go on about their business. By nightfall of an average courting day, a fiddler crab who has been standing on tiptoe for eight or ten hours waving a heavy claw in the air is in pretty sad shape. As in the case of the males of all species, however, he gets out of bed next morning, dashes some water on his face, and tries again.

Exercise

Thurber's style is highly idiomatic. The humor of the paragraph depends on his unexpected use of expressions not ordinarily associated with a discussion of the habits of shellfish. Identify at least ten of these expressions and be prepared to discuss their effectiveness.

A common characteristic of the Modern Style is the liberal coining and use of metaphors. There is a trendiness to the metaphorical style that can pall, but you ought to be aware of its popularity and of its limitations. The following two paragraphs are from Gail Sheehy's widely attacked and widely read treatise on life crises, *Passages*. Identify the metaphorical language and comment on its effectiveness.

The thought of death is too terrifying to confront head on, and so it keeps coming back in disguise; as pitching airplanes, swaying floors, precarious balconies, lovers' quarrels, mysterious backfires in our physical equipment. We elude it by pretending to function as before. Some people press down harder on the career accelerator. Others play more tennis, run more laps, give bigger parties, find younger flesh to take to bed.

What of the driven individual whose extreme path is an applauded one: Can he too be tripped up? The wunderkind hell-
bent on reaching his goal, having spent little time on building
emotional attachments, may ignore through his rocketing years
the hollow feeling inside the nose cone of his success. Society
goads him on. Or her—think of Dorothy Parker, Marilyn Mon-
roe, most movie queens for that matter. Having spent their ener-
gies on speeding along one narrow trajectory, the superachievers
may be shocked at the passage to midlife to find that they are
really behind. On the other hand, people who commit deeply to
a goal and play it out to their satisfaction sometimes flourish in
midlife when their neglected emotions are released. It can give
them a second lease on life.

What did you think of "wunderkind," "hell-bent" and the use of
the verb "commit" without the reflexive "themselves" after it?
Ms. Sheehy is also given to coining new words like "middles-
cence" (mid-life adolescence) and "sexicidal" (sexual suicide—or
what a way to go!), a gimmick you might be on the lookout for
in modern prose.

One characteristic that almost goes without mentioning in modern prose style is the use of shorter sentences and looser sentence
structure. Of course, because we are more used to reading modern
prose, it naturally seems easier for us to read. Only time will tell
how truly readable this writing is. Topicality alone may render
much of it impossibly obscure even with footnotes. This is already happening to Tom Wolfe, one of the century's most original stylists. A sociologist/anthropologist, Wolfe has staked out the
contemporary American behavioral scene. As the patriarch of the
so-called "new journalists" he has made his mark on contemporary prose by turning the language loose on a target and allowing
it to virtually absorb whatever it comes in contact with. He writes
prose with a camera eye, but it is an eye with a gleam in it.

The following paragraph is from Wolfe's account of a swanky
party given by Leonard Bernstein and his wife, Felicia, for the
Black Panthers. It is straight out of the sixties. Decide whether
you think it has retained its freshness or gone flat. Beyond that,

identify as many of Wolfe's verbal tricks as you can. Would the paragraph require any explanatory footnotes today?

Mmmmmmmmmmmmmmmmmmmmmmmmmmmmmmmmmmmm. These are nice. Little Roquefort cheese morsels rolled in crushed nuts. Very tasty. Very subtle. It's the way the dry sackiness of the nuts tiptoes up against the dour savor of the cheese that is so nice, so subtle. Wonder what the Black Panthers eat here on the hors d'oeuvre trail? Do the Panthers like little Roquefort cheese morsels rolled in crushed nuts this way, and asparagus tips in mayonnaise dabs, and *meatballs petites au Coq Hardi,* all of which are at this very moment being offered to them on gadrooned silver platters by maids in black uniforms with handironed white aprons. . . . The butler will bring them their drinks. . . . Deny it if you wish to, but such are the *pensées métaphysiques* that rush through one's head on these Radical Chic evenings just now in New York. For example, does that huge Black Panther there in the hallway, the one shaking hands with Felicia Bernstein herself, the one with the black leather coat and the dark glasses and the absolutely unbelievable Afro, Fuzzy-Wuzzy-scale, in fact—is he, a Black Panther, going on to pick up a Roquefort cheese morsel rolled in crushed nuts from off the tray, from a maid in uniform, and just pop it down the gullet without so much as missing a beat of Felicia's perfect Mary Astor voice. . . .

Here is an excerpt from Tom Wolfe's "O Rotten Gotham—Sliding Down into the Behavioral Sink," an article that is more durable perhaps because it deals with the enduring problem of limited space and cramped conditions and their effect on human survival. This excerpt is picked up in mid-sentence and carried to its frenetic conclusion. Notice the pile-driving momentum of Wolfe's prose and the way he makes use of whatever language is appropriate to involve the reader in the experience.

. . . working in cubicles with low ceilings and, often no access to a window, while construction crews all over Manhattan drive everybody up the Masonite wall with air-pressure generators with noises up to the boil-a-brain decibel levels, then rushing to get

home, piling into subways and trains, fighting for time and for
space, the usual day in New York—the whole now-normal thing
keeps shooting jolts of adrenalin into the body, breaking down
the body's defenses and winding up with the work-a-daddy human animal stroked out at the breakfast table with his head
apoplexed like a cauliflower out of his $6.95 semispread Pima-
cotton shirt, and nosed over into a plate of No-Kloresto egg substitute, signing off with the black thrombosis, cancer, kidney,
liver, or stomach failure, and the adrenals ooze to a halt, the size
of eggplants in July.

Wolfe's favorite trick is the accumulation of detail. He has an
uncanny eye (and ear) for the specific, and he overwhelms you
with dazzling lists of graphic items. It is for this very reason,
perhaps, that Tom Wolfe is suspended between stools: the social
scientists toss him to the literati, and the literati toss him to the
wolves (no pun intended). There exists, of course, a modern scientific style that is cooler than Wolfe's and that of most other
contemporary innovators. In fact, much important scientific information is currently being imparted in a plain, lucid, inoffen-
sive style that has developed in a direct line since the founding
of the Royal Academy of Science in the seventeenth century.

Here is a paragraph from an article by Lawrence Casler entitled
"This Thing Called Love Is Pathological." Its low-key treatment
of an emotionally charged subject is representative of the clear-
headed style of much contemporary scientific commentary. If those
who complain that writing is in the doldrums have not yet revised their thinking, let them heed Casler's controlled and pleas-
ing style. Part of this excerpt is presented in an altered format so
that certain stylistic techniques will be more obvious.

Love, like other emotions, has
    causes,
    characteristics
    and consequences.
Temporarily setting aside an inquiry into why, or whether, love
    makes the world go 'round,

makes life worth living,
     and conquers all,
let us consider the somewhat more manageable question
     of causality.
Love between man and woman has many determinants, but instinct is not one of them. Anthropologists have described entire societies in which love is absent, and there are many individuals in our society who have never loved. To argue that such societies and individuals are "sick" or "the exception that proves the rule" (whatever *that* means) is sheer arrogance. Love, when it exists, is a learned emotion. Explanation for its current prevalence must be sought elsewhere than in the genes.

Admittedly, Casler reaches into no new bag of tricks for his effects. He likes triads and alliteration ("causes, characteristics, and consequences"), he is comfortable with familiar imagery, he dislikes cant. It is what he doesn't do that distinguishes him as a writer of clean prose. He isn't cute. He doesn't pull punches. He doesn't "milk a metaphor" or "run a cliché into the ground." When he gets to his point, and he gets there quickly, he makes it simply and directly: "Love, when it exists, is a learned emotion."

Later in the same essay, he responds to that persistent modern worry about selfishness in the same cool and compelling manner.

Would the love-free person be egotistical? Perhaps, but only if that term is relieved of its ugly connotations. To be self-centered does not mean to disregard the worth of other people. It does imply that other people are reacted to within a frame of reference that is centered on the self. There is nothing reprehensible about this. In fact, most psychologists would probably accept the position that we are *all* self-centered. No matter how other directed our actions may appear, they are functions of *our* perception of the world, based, in turn, on *our* previous experience. Since every act is a "self-ish" one, evaluative criteria should be applied only to the effects of selfishness, rather than to selfishness per se.

We have to be on guard, of course, against the willingness to believe. When Casler says, "There is nothing reprehensible about this," do we sit back and take his word for it? How much stock do we place in the fact that "most psychologists" accept the position that we are *all* self-centered? We also have to take note of certain fashionable words ("frame of reference," "other directed," "perception," "evaluative criteria," even "per se") but these words are as much a part of our contemporary baggage as such common words as "felicity," "agreeable," "taking the air," and "countenance" were to the Augustans. It is easy to like or dislike a style because of the content it encloses. Examine your own reaction to what little you have seen of this essay on love. Do you think that it's possible for a writer to be too reasonable for his own good?

Richard A. Lanham, author of *Style: An Anti-textbook,* thinks so and has this to say about contemporary efforts to promote what he calls "the dogma of clarity."

What we have now is a tedious, repetitive, unoriginal body of dogma—clarity, sincerity, plainness, duty—tarted up every week in a new, disposable paperback dress. The dogma of clarity . . . is based on a false theory of knowledge; its scorn of ornament, on a misleading taxonomy of style; the frequent exhortations to sincerity, on a naive theory of the self; and the unctuous moralizing, on a Boy Scout didacticism. Instruction in style ought to concentrate on what can be taught. Goethe, in his conversations with Eckermann, is reputed to have said that "if any man would write in a noble style let him first possess a noble soul." Wonderful, but not much help. It may be, though some wise men have denied it, that virtue can be taught, but it seems unlikely that it can be taught in Freshman Composition. Nor sincerity. Nor spontaneity. Nor true grit. What can be taught is words. And they must be taught in the full matrix of human utterance, written and spoken, accompanied by a theory of style equally broad. A student bright enough to be taught style needs a context for it beyond didactic precept, an intelligible and sound context. Style cannot be taught only by lists of self-contradicting proverbs, strings of do's and don'ts. Students so instructed are not being taught; they are being housebroken.

Exercise

Analyze Lanham's style in this paragraph. You know enough about style at this point to be able to make some cogent judgments. How "elevated" is his own style? Does he use any familiar tricks? any unfamiliar ones? Is he readable? Does he make sense? Can you paraphrase his philosophy? Is what he suggests of any practical help? Does this book redress any of his grievances? Has your own philosophy of composition changed by now?

There is an energy and vitality, an inventiveness and a sense of fun about so much of the prose that has been written in modern times. Perhaps what stands out most about the Modern Style is the fact that it can be simple without being silly. Borrowing from recent slang, one could label it "laid back," for it is a style that winks at itself and figures anything's worth a try. Its dominant influence has been journalism, as the line between novelist and journalist has continued to blur (or be smudged, whichever you prefer).

What the future holds for English prose style is (or very well could be) up to you.

VI

Transactions

A good writer looks upon writing as a transaction between writer and reader in which the reader puts his trust in the writer and the writer honors that trust. Someone once said that the reader ought to feel "safe" in the hands of the author. It is this sense of security that forms the bond good writers hope to establish between themselves and their audiences. Even though readers can sometimes be willing victims of bad style, it is the duty of the writer who hopes to write truly well to resist the temptation to humor that weakness. Giving them what they want is never justification for selling them, or yourself, short.

Good writers value integrity and self-respect. They refuse to settle for a style that is superficially clever or charming at the expense of honesty of purpose. To "proper words" in "proper places" must be added "proper ends." All the great stylists from Milton to Mencken have honored this principle because they knew that even the most polished style will tarnish when exposed to the corrosion of deceit.

233

In the last section you saw how potentially good style could be corrupted by questionable motives. In this section you will see how that potential can be realized when style is used in good faith.

The four basic styles presented in this section pretty well cover the range of stylistic options available to you. It might help if you think of them as primary colors from which you can derive your own mixes and shadings.

The first style is the Plain Style. This is a fairly common style, popular with most contemporary writers. It favors simple language and simple sentences. It is an unadorned style, good for transmitting information or clarifying concepts. Although it is not necessarily a personal style, it is informal enough to reveal the personality of the writer. Its simplicity, by the way, is deceptive. To write with economy and not sacrifice grace is an art indeed.

Contrary to the Plain Style is the Grand Style, a style in which sophisticated language and sentence structure are used to express matters of gravity or complexity in a formal and impersonal manner. Although it is easy to abuse this style by becoming pompous or vague, writers who can handle it like to use it when they have important statements to make and want to make sure that they will be taken seriously. It is an elegant style which, under control, can be quite compelling and impressive.

The Running Style is the style of the writer who thinks his subject through as he is in the process of writing about it and who likes to keep the juices flowing with a minimum of interruption. It is a flowing, open style that relies mainly upon simple language and almost exclusively on extensive use of loose sentences. Although it can quickly become chatty and verbose in unskilled hands, it can, when used wisely, reveal a probing mind intelligently absorbed in a topic and actively at work examining that topic. Usually, the writer who employs the Running Style has a fairly good idea of where he is going, but he's not quite sure how he's going to get there until he's on his way. He may muse, wonder, question, "think out loud," as he feels his way along.

The last style to be considered in this section is the Ironic Style. This is the style that pits form against content in order to add a dimension to what is being said. Basically, it has to do with expressing your attitude toward something in a contradictory manner either by treating a serious matter lightly or a ridiculous matter seriously. Incidental methods of achieving ironic effect are the "poker-faced lie" that reveals a sober truth, the humorous half-truth that betrays a not so funny whole truth, and oversentimentalization of the trivial. In addition to being the traditional technique of satire, the Ironic Style is excellent writing practice because it demands the highest sensitivity to the relationship between form, content, and audience.

These four styles form the basis for developing a style that reflects your personality and, at the same time, respects your audience. Try, as you work with them, to put into practice all you have learned about word usage, sentence structure, paragraph harmony, and, above all, your obligation to honesty and fair play.

Because you will be dealing with each of these four styles in unadulterated doses, you may find the effect somewhat overwhelming. Rarely does a writer sit down and say to himself, "Today I think I will write in the Plain Style" (or the Grand Style or whatever), and never would he restrict himself to a single style for an extended period of time or to accomplish a variety of writing tasks—*unless* he were either writing this book or learning from it.

A style can begin to feel like a pointless parody of itself if you work with it too long at a stretch. If you feel this happening to you, move around among the various styles—or take a break—until you can regain perspective. Practice at anything is self-conscious, and the danger is always there that you will become restless and skeptical from too much looking over your own shoulder. Just remember that periodic bouts of intense concentration on any technique of style will lead to mastery of that technique and ultimately to mastery of style in general.

22. The Plain Style

The first thing that has to be said about the Plain Style is that it is not as easy to write in as it looks. It is much easier, in fact, to be long-winded and grandiose and write sentences in which the clauses and phrases pile up, the diction becomes inflated, and the content gets quietly lost in a maze of qualifiers, repetitions, and uncertain references. Ernest Hemingway has told of how much work went into making his prose sound effortless. The truth is that the simplest way to say something is seldom the first way that comes to mind.

Because the Plain Style lacks the adornment that can conceal flaws in diction and syntax, it makes greater demands on the writer to choose his words carefully and construct his sentences meticulously. The hallmark of the Plain Style is simplicity. Its language is Anglo-Saxon, and its sentences, while not exclusively "simple," are basically uncomplicated. The problem such simplicity poses for the writer is that he must try not to sound stupid or boring—or merely silly.

The Plain Style is a highly visible style; it shows its warts and blemishes. For this reason extensive revision is usually necessary before it sounds pleasingly plain. The catch here is that in the process of simplifying the vocabulary and syntax, you may oversimplify the content. Although the Plain Style is the best style to use for simple ideas, the ideas need not necessarily be simple. In fact, the writer who can communicate a complex idea in a simple way, without oversimplifying, has truly mastered the art of style. It is the nature, not the complexity, of the subject matter that determines which style you will choose to write in.

Tone is also an important consideration in the selection of a style appropriate to the nature of the subject matter. If you need to be grave or wish to be ironic, you would not use the Plain Style, for the tone of the Plain Style is generally lighter, more matter-of-fact. You might use it, for example, in writing up the minutes of a meeting but not in a letter of commendation for distinguished service.

Example 1
Analyze the diction, sentence structure, and tone of the following paragraph.

Deregulation of the airlines has caused serious problems. Increased competition has forced some companies out of business and has sharply reduced the profits of others. Customers, too, have suffered. Overbooking to assure full loads has left some passengers stranded in terminals adding to the congestion already created by confusing schedules and frequent delays. It would seem that lower rates are a mixed blessing. You can get there cheaper these days, but getting there is no longer half the fun. It's no fun at all.

There are seven sentences in this paragraph, most of them short and simple. However, the length is varied enough to avoid monotony. The very short third sentence, for example, is followed by the longest sentence in the paragraph, a sentence which, coming as it does in the middle, provides a fulcrum for the shorter sentences on either side.

Exercise 1
1. What effect do words like "suffered," "stranded," and "cheaper" have in this context?

2. How do the last two sentences determine the tone of this paragraph?
3. Write a similar paragraph on one of these topics: oil prices; interest rates; tuition; foreign competition; the job market; inflation.

Example 2
Notice how the first four sentences of the following paragraph merely reinforce the main idea. This sort of redundancy is permissible when the purpose is to simulate through writing the way something might actually feel: in this case, the mounting pressure of irresistible hunger.

Did you ever give in to a junk food attack? It's a craving that cannot be denied. The harder you try to resist it, the stronger it gets. One moment you're a normal human being with normal appetites, the next you're a madman who can only be pacified with Oreos or Twinkies or taco-flavored, pizza-glazed, cheese-dipped, french-fried corn chips. As Oscar Wilde so fetchingly said, "The only way to overcome temptation is to yield to it." Better fat and placid than skinny and mean.

Again, the longest sentence is in the middle giving balance to the paragraph. It may be long, but it is by no means difficult or complex. Its length is the result of a deliberate piling up of modifiers calculated to cater to the corrupt tastes of the most depraved junk food junkies.

Exercise 2
1. In sentence 1, why "give in" instead of "surrender"?
2. Identify the use of assonance in the last sentence and comment on its effectiveness.
3. Write a similar paragraph on one of the following topics: soap operas; old movies; scruffy clothes; cutting class; speeding; being the life of the party; teasing; practical joking.

Example 3
The following paragraph on sales says a lot in a few words. Notice the simplicity of the language and the sentence structure.

Sales are irresistible. When prices plummet, willpower withers. And sales junkies are not the only ones who come running. Even those who brag about their sales resistance have their price. A coat you wouldn't touch at $300 suddenly looks good at $225 and even better at $200. At $150 you'd kill for it, and at $100 you'd gladly die for it. That the price tag is pure fiction doesn't faze you in the least. If it's "marked down," it's bound to be a bargain. Of course, once your resistance is down, all is lost. You need shoes to match that coat and a purse to match those shoes. Who cares if those items are overpriced? Look at what you saved on the coat!

These twelve simple-looking sentences are not really all that simple. After the opening sentence (the only truly "simple" one), it's hard to find a sentence that doesn't have either a subordinate clause, a relative clause, or a noun clause. And only two or three sentences start right off with the subject.

Exercise 3

1. Pick out examples of alliteration. Are they justified? Do they work?
2. Analyze sentences 5 and 6. What idiomatic tricks are used to get the price and response from a negative $300 to a positive $100?
3. Write a similar paragraph on one of the following topics: eavesdropping; peeking; spying; coveting; showing off; gossiping; overeating.

Example 4

Here is a brief observation on a familiar daily occurrence. In nine compact sentences a situation is presented, illustrated, and put into sympathetic perspective.

Being caught in the middle is never a pleasant experience. In some occupations, however, there is no easy way out of this dilemma. Take the case of the clerk in a dress shop. On one side of her stands the supervisor prodding her to go after the customers. On the other side stands a customer who resents being bothered while she is "just looking." What can the poor clerk do? If she is

rebuffed after a mild "May I help you?" she can feel the eyes of
the supervisor warning her not to give up. But if she pushes an
item or stands guard as the customer goes through the racks, she
may lose a sale. It's a brave clerk who can ignore the threat of an
overbearing supervisor. Most would rather risk offending the
customer than alienating the boss. It's something to think about
the next time you're in a store and a clerk annoys you.

Variety is achieved in this paragraph by the use of parallel phrases
(sentences 3 and 4), a question (sentence 5), the use of phrases
familiar to shoppers ("just looking," "May I help you?"), and
parallel subordinate clauses (sentences 6 and 7).

Exercise 4
1. What is the function of "however" in the second sentence?
2. How can you justify beginning sentence 7 with a coordinating
   conjunction? How does the word "but" really function in this
   context?
3. Write a similar paragraph on one of the following topics: di-
   vided loyalties; triangular love affairs; conflicting invitations;
   differing parents; equal but incompatible temptations.

Example 5
In this paragraph a common assumption about common sense is
refuted and the refutation convincingly illustrated all within the
space of fourteen fairly short sentences. Notice that it is the very
terseness of the style that contributes to the clarity and impact of
the paragraph.

Common sense, they say, is not so common. If few use it, the
argument goes, few must have it. This is a questionable assumption. You can have something and still not use it. While use presumes possession, possession does not presume use. What's
probably true is that common sense is common enough, it just
gets overlooked. Faced with complicated problems, we expect
complicated solutions. Such is not necessarily the case. Take ap-
pliances, for example. Because most of us do not bother to un-

derstand how they work, we panic when they break down. If the vacuum sweeper won't run, we don't think to check the plug. If the washing machine overflows, we don't think to check the drain. Not all causes of breakdowns are that simple, but most are simpler than we think. Next time the furnace won't come on, use your common sense and check out the pilot light before calling an expensive repairman.

Sentences 2, 5, and 7 use repetition for conciseness and impact. Sentence 5 is also a good example of antithetical construction (see pp. 106–107). The word "panic" in sentence 10 compresses much meaning into a short space because it connotes not only fearful confusion but also the feelings of ignorance and helplessness, frustration and bewilderment that accompany irritating and mysterious happenings.

Exercise 5
1. Can you identify examples of parallel construction? Why is it used where it is?
2. How is sentence variety achieved? Identify several different sentence structures.
3. Write a similar paragraph on one of the following topics: book learning; the school of hard knocks; victims of circumstances; the golden mean; rainy day reserves; safety in numbers.

Example 6
Here is a trivial little commentary on coathangers, perfectly suited to the light touch of the Plain Style.

Wire coathangers are a menace to civilized behavior. No sooner do two of them even come near one another on a rack than they get tangled together like antsy teenagers. If you do manage to separate one of them, the other one invariably falls to the floor. In a cluster they defy the most adroit attempts at extraction. Even that one that looks suspiciously free at first glance will, at first tug, lock itself in a huddle with the rest of the gang. It's enough to make strong men weep. A pre-dawn skirmish with the hateful hanger has been known to corrupt the gentlest natures, turning

judges into hangmen, ministers into monsters, and sending professors on flunking sprees. Let's beat the bloody things into hooks
and screw them into the wall. That ought to keep them in their
place.

The exaggeration in the first sentence establishes the humorous
tone of the paragraph. Likewise, the mildly inflated diction in
sentence 4 (adroit, extraction) is in deliberate contradiction to the
trivial subject matter and thus reinforces the humorous tone.
Words like "antsy," "tug," "huddle," "gang," "skirmish,"
"flunking," "bloody," and "screw" go to the opposite extreme
and counterbalance the effect of the elevated language. While the
style is still plain, the language is intentionally uneven, although
there is no word here that comes even close to being difficult to
understand. Notice again the use of a short sentence (6) followed
by a much longer one (7) and the way the short sentence prepares
you for the particulars of the long one.

Exercise 6

1. Identify the simple sentences in this paragraph and analyze
   their locations. Study the relationship between all the sentences.
2. Identify instances of the use of alliteration (there are at least
   seven) and discuss their effect, whether good or bad, on the
   tone and overall effectiveness of the paragraph. What is the
   purpose of repeating "first" in the expressions "first glance"
   and "first tug"?
3. Write a similar paragraph on one of the following topics:
   toothpaste tubes; curtain rods; shoe laces; garden hoses; de-
   cals; Christmas trees.

Example 7

Here is a new look at an old expression. Notice how much background, speculation, and commentary is contained within the
paragraph; yet the paragraph does not seem compressed.

The expression "banker's hours" is a curious one. Way back when most banks opened around ten and closed by two-thirty, word got around that bankers worked only four or five hours a day with at least an hour off for lunch. Not only that, they were privileged to arrive late and leave early. Hence the expression "banker's hours" came to be applied to anyone who worked a short day or who came in late or went home early. In reality, bankers had to arrive much earlier, stay much later, and work much longer than those hours the bank was open for business; but the public believed only what it saw. Today, with banks open all hours, the original meaning of the phrase should be obsolete. Nevertheless, the phrase remains in our vocabulary, its original meaning intact, and is used by persons who would not be able to tell you where it came from. Just try going in late some morning or leaving early some afternoon and see if someone doesn't yell out, "Banker's hours!" When that happens, don't stop to explain. Remember, now that banks are automated, there may be truth after all in the expression.

The use of transitional words and expressions is one device used in this paragraph to make it feel less crowded ("Not only that," "Hence," "In reality," "Nevertheless," "Remember"). Another device is the use of longer, but not necessarily more complex, sentences which add flow to the paragraph.

Exercise 7

1. Why does sentence 3 need sentence 2? What is the function of "not only that"?
2. Which is the topic sentence? Does it work well where it is, or would it work better somewhere else? Explain "should be."
3. Write a similar paragraph on one of the following expressions: "better late than never"; "waste not, want not"; "absence makes the heart grow fonder"; "it's the exception that proves the rule."

There is a classic purity to the Plain Style. It is a style shorn of excess, trimmed clean of overstatement. It is a polished style, and as you now know, that polish requires considerable rubbing. Someone once said that it takes time to be brief. Anyone who has ever tried to write a ten-word telegram knows this is true. While the Plain Style is not the telegraphic style, both insist that every word count. When you can make every word count, you know what it means to have "a way with words."

23. The Grand Style

The Grand Style is the style appropriate to matters of seriousness and significance. It is used to heighten the effect of the subject matter by means of elevated language and more elaborate sentence structure. It is the style of great oratory, of eulogy, and of declarations of high purpose and intent. It favors Latinate word usage and the employment of periodic and balanced sentences. Its rhythms are stately, and its tone is often solemn, always sincere.

What the Grand Style is *not* is pompous or stilted, wordy or vague. It is not a cocoon of fancy rhetoric wrapped around a worm of foolish thought. Because it is so often abused, it is important that you get it straight and do it right; for, as you already know, it is very easy to let sound get in the way of sense and allow the construction of intricate sentences to get out of hand. The Grand Style is not rhetoric at the expense of reason. When used properly, it lends a profound tone to a profound topic.

Example 1
Pay close attention to the diction used in the following eulogy. Although it is sober, it is simpler than you might expect.

The university community was immeasurably saddened by the news of the passing of one of its most distinguished founders,

245

Mr. Russell Coleman, a man dedicated to the advancement of education and devoted to the institution of which he was so much a part and to which he gave so much of himself. It is all too seldom that we are privileged to be acquainted with the quality of spirit and the generous nature that characterized this fine man. Ever eager to give of himself, ever willing to make sacrifices in the name of a cause in which he so totally believed, Russell Coleman deserves to be remembered as the courageous and selfless man he was and to be praised for his tireless labors on behalf of this university. It is with heavy hearts that we mourn his departure, knowing full well that his loss will be sorely felt among all who were fortunate enough to enjoy his company and that it will be a long time before we shall see his like again. To Russell Coleman, our gratitude and our farewell.

Only poets like Milton and Keats can get away with eulogies of great originality. Ordinarily, audiences expect to hear certain language used (distinguished, dedicated, devoted, courageous, selfless, tireless), but they will not accept a string of simple sentences that turn a eulogy into a multiple-choice test. In this paragraph, the sentence structure provides the proper setting for those routine words, a setting that makes them sound sincere, even fresh. The opening sentence makes use of an appositive and two parallel constructions (dedicated to . . . devoted to; of which . . . to which). The opening clause of sentence 3, with its parallels (Ever eager . . . ever willing), leads grandly up to the man's name, after which another set of parallels (to be remembered . . . to be praised) leads grandly away from it. The last sentence is as brief and smart as a salute.

Exercise 1

1. What other words and phrases common to eulogies can you identify in this paragraph? Do you feel their use is justified? If not, how would you rewrite them?
2. Analyze the rhythm and sound effects and determine their contribution to the tone.
3. Write a similar paragraph befitting one of the following situ-

ations: the bestowing of an award; a ground breaking ceremony; a retirement; the giving of a large donation; the saving of a life.

Example 2

Money is never a laughing matter, and the more money involved, the more call for the Grand Style. Notice how seriously the situation is taken in the following paragraph.

Improprieties in the distribution of research grants have prompted influential donors to reexamine the nature of their charitable appropriations and reconsider the wisdom of their bequests. Dismayed by the complaints of qualified but disappointed candidates and unsettled by repeated allegations of blatant discrimination, many people in a position to contribute generously to the advancement of scholarly efforts in science and the humanities are reluctant to participate in an endeavor that might reflect unfavorably upon them. These people are eager to offer their assistance, but they are not prepared to be embarrassed by administrative injustices. Before they withdraw their support altogether, it would behoove those with whom rests the task of recruitment and dissemination of financial contributions to initiate a thorough investigation of the funding process and of all personnel directly involved in it.

The uneasy donors pass between the twin pillars of "re-examine" and "reconsider" to arrive at the threatening conclusion to this periodic sentence: the implied withdrawal of their "bequests." The second sentence portends doom with its opening parallel participial phrases (Dismayed by . . . unsettled by) and its death-knell alliteration (Dismayed, disappointed, discrimination). In four somber sentences, the problem is stated and the ultimatum given. There is no nonsense about the gravity of this situation, and the style only darkens the colors.

Exercise 2

1. A proliferation of words ending in "tion" usually signals an increase in the level of abstraction. There are seven "tion"

words in the paragraph. How do you judge their effect? Are
there any you would replace with appropriate synonyms?

2. To get a feeling for the effect of diction on tone and style,
   replace the words in the left column with the synonyms in the
   right:

improprieties	hanky-panky
charitable appropriations	tax write-offs
dismayed	ticked off
unsettled	bugged
reflect unfavorably	backfire
injustices	hijinx
behoove	be smart of
recruitment and dissemination	getting and giving
initiate a thorough investigation	check out

3. Write a similar paragraph on one of the following topics:
   drugstore kickbacks; rebates; welfare fraud; payola; profit taking; mark-ups.

Example 3

Here is a short paragraph expressing a passionate moral sentiment. Even though it includes some very short sentences, the
style is still grand. See why.

"The sanctity of life" becomes a sanctimonious cliché in the
mouth of a leader who knows at the very moment he is uttering
such a pious pronouncement that his country's prisons are filled
to overflowing with victims of his own repression. How easily
such a phrase rises to the lips of a man like this, a man to whom
the only life that is sacred is his own, a man to whom the lives
of others are important only insofar as they can be of use to him.
Here is a man who promises everything and grants nothing. He
promises protection. He promises sustenance. He promises glory.
But his protection is better refused, his gifts better rejected, his
glory better renounced. He is the arch hypocrite in whose mouth
the word "life" means certain death.

The tone of this paragraph is one of controlled rage. A simpler or looser style could never contain the scorn, and unless it is contained, the paragraph might sound merely shrill. Balance and restraint preserve the delicate harmony between style and meaning.

Exercise 3

1. Why not begin sentence 2 like this: "Such a phrase rises easily to the lips . . ."? What difference would there be in effect?
2. The five sentences before the last could have been compressed into one: "Here is a man who offers protection, sustenance, and glory, but it is better not to accept them." What is the difference in impact between the sentences as written and the revision? What accounts for the difference? How much does punctuation have to do with it?
3. Write a similar paragraph in which you put one of the following sayings into the wrong mouth:

     "Money can't buy happiness."   a millionaire
     "Let them eat cake!"   Head of HEW
     "two cars in every garage"   import dealer
     "Power to the people!"   USSR party chief

Example 4

Here is a short essay written in the Grand Style. It is a serious and strongly held statement of opinion about freedom. Notice how language and sentence structure cooperate to maintain the intensity and the sincerity of the sentiment expressed and create a moment that marches toward a relentless conclusion.

Freedom

It is a violation of integrity and an outrage to dignity when, in return for the paltry munificence of the State, a man forfeits his precious freedom. Such a man receives little and sacrifices much, for there can be no assessing of freedom in terms of worldly chattel. Nothing imaginable is compensation sufficient to warrant the squandering of man's noblest yearning and most dearly defended right.

It is not man's intelligence but his capacity for freedom that distinguishes him from the animals. While it may be curiously comforting to some to think of wild animals as being "born free," it is manifestly obvious to others that animals are the slaves of instinct and that their greatest desire is to behave according to those instincts. If they crave any freedom at all, it is the license to indulge the physical hungers those instincts arouse. Freedom for man, however, is the freedom to satisfy spiritual hungers, to transcend instinct, to unfetter himself from the tyranny of biological restraints and assert his independence. It is because freedom is so often inimical to comfort and complacency that it is so frequently and viciously repressed by those who fear that it will interfere with the soulless utopias that deluded men devise for the maintaining of perfect order and the establishment of systems of political stagnation.

If freedom is a delusion, then it is a grand one; if it is a dream, then it is a magnificent one; if it is madness, then it is the madness of divinest sense. To surrender it voluntarily is to enter willingly into bondage from which there is no deliverance and in which the human spirit must surely decay and die.

It is style that carries the opening paragraph, for each sentence is merely a variation on the same theme: freedom is too valuable to sell. The opening sentence is periodic, holding the point in suspense until the end and thus setting the tone for the entire essay. Balance characterizes sentence 2, paragraph 2 (comforting to some . . . obvious to others); sentence 4, paragraph 2 (to satisfy . . . to transcend . . . to unfetter); and the "if . . . then" construction of the opening sentence of paragraph 3. The infinitive noun clauses and parallel "which" phrases of the last sentence reinforce the gravity of the statement, as do the Biblical tone of "surely" and the alliterative "decay and die."

Exercise 4

1. What are some informal synonyms for the following words and phrases used in this essay:

    forfeits
    receives little and sacrifices much
    compensation sufficient
    distinguishes
    unfetter
    inimical

2. The phrase, in the last sentence of paragraph 2, "by those who *fear* that it will inter*fere*" is weakened by the unintentional rhyme. Can you find a substitute for one or both words?

3. Write a similar short essay on one of the following topics: reputation; amateur standing; respect; love; character; personality; talent.

The Grand Style is an impressive style, and when it is used wisely, it can add dignity and power to a topic about which you feel deeply. Although you will see later how it can be used ironically, ordinarily it is used soberly as a means of letting the reader sense the extent of your involvement and gauge the quality of your concern.

24. The Running Style

The Running Style could be described as a "thinking out loud" style. It is used when you get hold of a topic that is somewhat elusive and you want to ramble on about it, figuring out as you go where it is you are going and just what it is you think. This does not mean that you haven't thought at all about the topic before or that you lack sufficient knowledge to discuss it. What it means is that you know that somewhere in the back of your mind an opinion is forming and you want both you and your reader to explore the thought process by which you arrive at that opinion. The approach is philosophical, not argumentative, although you may certainly arrive at a controversial conclusion. The point, however, is the journey, not the destination.

The reasoning at work in the Running Style is inductive rather than deductive. Whereas with the Plain, Grand, and Ironic styles you begin with a conclusion you have drawn and use it as a thesis to be defended and applied as a principle, with the Running Style you begin with a question in your mind about something you have wondered about or observed and then, in the process of trying to answer it or simply make sense out of it, you arrive finally at a conclusion, however tentative.

The Running Style requires much skill because it is fraught

with much danger. In the hands of the naive, it can easily get out of control or serve merely as an excuse to drift aimlessly and write carelessly. Just as it takes a trained musician to improvise successfully or an accomplished poet to handle free verse well, it takes a confident writer to sustain the Running Style without getting lost in ambiguity, bad grammar, awkward sentence structure, and general confusion. The ideal result of this style is a rough draft that doesn't sound like a rough draft. Since too much revision or rewriting can spoil the spontaneity that is the charm of the Running Style, the writer who employs it must give a virtuoso performance in which he thinks well and writes well simultaneously.

The language of the Running Style is closer to that of the Plain Style than to the Grand Style, and it is wise to keep the language fairly simple as a way of avoiding the vagueness this style is susceptible to. What mainly differentiates this style from the others is its extensive use of the *loose* sentence. Sentences tend to be long, but their length is the result of the running together of independent phrases and clauses connected by simple coordinating or subordinating conjunctions or joined by commas rather than the use of convoluted structures. The point of view is usually subjective, and the topics are likely to be of personal rather than public interest. Your purpose is not to explain a position or argue a point but to share a response, to invite the reader into your mind and try to make the visit worthwhile. The Running Style is suited to this purpose because it pulls the reader along with a minimum of interruption.

Example 1
What is consciousness and who has it has been hotly debated. Here, in a short paragraph, is an attempt to think it through.

It could be nothing more than the slant of the sun, a patch of fog, a rainbow in an oil slick that switches the channels of the mind and transports you with the speed of light to a prior emotion, and with a rush, a long-forgotten feeling is as new as now, fresh and familiar, yet at the same time curiously remote, as if you can actually feel yourself feeling, so that in the same moment you are both here and there, time is both then and now, and you know in a flash that to be human is to be conscious, conscious in a way you are sure no animal could ever be, not with all its celebrated cunning and intelligence and its occasional apparent departures from instinct when it behaves in a way we like to describe as "almost human." If that were consciousness, then we would be trapped in that consciousness, never aware of it at all, never even thinking about the fact that others are conscious, too, taking it supremely for granted and going on about the business of survival as if that were absolutely all that mattered, and we would have to invent a new word to describe our brand of consciousness which is not "almost" anything. But we are truly conscious because we have not only the ability to know but to know that we know, and the difference that makes is vast and well-nigh imponderable; for when we are able to monitor our own minds, to change them, turn them around, redirect their attention, and know all the time that we are doing this, then do we understand how it came to pass that we and we alone invented language which is both tool and proof of the magnificent gift of consciousness.

The "running" quality of the first sentence is achieved by the use of phrases in a series (slant . . . patch . . . rainbow; you are . . . time is . . . you know), coordinating conjunctions (and, yet, and), subordinate clauses (as if . . . so that . . . when it . . .), prepositional phrases (with a rush . . . not with all), and qualifying phrases of various natures (fresh and familiar, conscious in a way). The last sentence makes good use of coordination (But, and, for, and) and of infinitive phrases (to change, turn, redirect, know) to maintain flow.

Exercise 1
1. Analyze the structure of the second sentence. Rewrite it in a series of simple sentences.

2. Can you think of a better metaphor than "switches the channels"? What effect on the tone do the phrases "it came to pass"
   and "magnificent gift" have?
3. Write a similar paragraph in which you "think out loud" about
   one of the following topics: conscience; habit; taste; memory;
   dreams.

Example 2

In the following paragraph random impressions are gathered together and set down in a way that suggests the process whereby
latent thoughts are forced to the surface and conclusions drawn.

Surely the world of modern art is awash with confused excitement, and the ignorant wander through it with glazed eyes and
furrowed brows, lost in doubt about its honesty and their own
taste, fearful of seeming gullible if they are being made fools of
or of seeming boorish if they are not. Where can they turn for
help? Not certainly to the artist who has assumed a take-it-or-
leave-it attitude and has no patience with those who ask, "What
does it mean" or "What is it supposed to represent?" since, of
course, he would, if he were inclined to answer at all, deign to
tell you that there are no answers to your questions, that your
questions are meaningless. "Why should art mean anything?" he
would say, or "What in the world does "meaning" mean?" And
so they, the innocently ignorant, stumble on, in embarrassed
skepticism, looking inside themselves for answers to questions
they dare not ask but which swim unbidden into their minds,
and, finding still only mystery and doubt, tiptoe silently away,
clutching their wise misgivings to their bosoms, suspecting in
their hearts that "where nothing can be seen, nothing is."

This attack on modern art could have been bitter and antago-
nistic. As it is, the tone is more one of impatience; disdain for
the artist is tempered with sympathy for the viewer. Moreover,
there is the suggestion beneath it all that cowardly viewers invite
exploitation by unscrupulous artists.

Exercise 2

1. What effect does the short second sentence have on the paragraph? What about the quotations? Would they be better as paraphrases?
2. Which words tie this paragraph down and keep it from becoming abstract? Would you make any changes?
3. Write a similar paragraph in which you speculate on one of the following cultural clichés: theatre is superior to film; film is superior to TV; bestsellers are usually junk; rock is schlock; figure skating is merely flashy; America has no composers; the BBC can do no wrong; only PBS has any claim to quality.

Example 3

Here is an intensely personal revelation and a good example of how effective the Running Style can be in contributing to the atmosphere and conveying a mood.

Sometimes I pretend that I am invisible, and even though I know that I am not, I can fool myself—and I like to think, others—into thinking that for a while nobody can see me as I pass by them or move among them watching them flicker by like shadows, unaware that I am in their midst, spying on them. But I am not a voyeur when I observe them, for I do not look for secrets or strange behavior, and I do not really care that much about them as individuals at all. As a matter of fact, it is more important to me that I cannot be seen than that I can look at them unmolested, since what seems to motivate me is a craving for anonymity, not curiosity, not the answer to any questions I might have about them but rather the feeling that I will not be accosted, disturbed, required to do anything, that I can glide along suspended for a time, perfectly free of the prison of my body or the madhouse of my emotions; for I experience neither physical nor emotional sensations when I am invisible. What I do feel, if indeed it can even be called feeling, is a release of the spirit, as if all experience is transmitted through a window of serene and perfect consciousness, uncluttered by aches of anger, hunger, or nerves, receptive in a detached way to the sights and sounds and smells which surround me but do not penetrate me. I do not have to respond or be responded to. I can stare into display cases without being asked to buy, stand idly on a corner and not be considered vagrant, wander about in circles without appearing odd, drift along a damp street under misty lamps and not feel the pavement or the cold. I sit alone in a dark and vacant movie house watching imitations of life stuck in time, and as I huddle in my coat and pull my collar snugly around my neck, it is not to warm me but to protect me, to reassure me that inside the coat you see on me there is no me inside to see.

Verbs are important in heightening the effect of this paragraph. In addition to the verbs of vision (see, watch, observe, look, spy) there are several verbs, especially toward the end, that reinforce the lonely mood of this psychological narrative (glide, stare, stand, wander, drift, sit alone, pass by, huddle, warm me, protect me, reassure me).

Exercise 3

1. Analyze the sentence structure. What maintains the momentum? What is the function of the shortest sentence ("I do not have to respond or be responded to")?
2. What words best describe the tone of this paragraph? Find reasons in the diction and syntax.
3. Write a similar paragraph either on one of the suggested topics or on one that comes from your own personal experience: a feeling of being outside yourself; a sense of déjà vu; a sense of unreality; a sense of disorientation; a mystical experience; a sense of destiny; a sense of foreboding; clairvoyance; mental telepathy.

Example 4

The following is a complete essay in the Running Style. Here the writer, intrigued by a widespread fascination with clocks, discovers, in the process of writing about them, some interesting thoughts about them and about what they measure. Notice how increasingly philosophical the essay becomes. This is an example of the mind working from a casual observation to a serious conclusion in the very act of writing.

As Time Goes By

Some people are fascinated by clocks, obsessed with them as a matter of fact, and even go so far as to form clubs and hold conventions where they display not only antique clocks but clocks the members themselves have painstakingly assembled from scratch. The ones they seem to prefer are those clocks with all their innards showing, wheels spinning, bars moving up and down, things ticking and chiming and wheezing and gonging, bizarre mutants of those charming old golden wedding clocks our grandparents had with clockworks of gold sealed in glass globes and wound up only once every fifty years or so. Those charming old clocks lulled you into thinking time could stand still instead of reminding you that time is racing by and your life along with it.

Possessed by the phenomenon of the passage of time, these clockmongers delight in rigging up toothy wheels that clack away every second like a heartbeat, never letting you forget that even while you're not looking, your life is growing shorter at a relentlessly steady pace. Maybe they like to torture themselves with these *memento mori* the way philosophers used to keep skulls by their sides and monks used to sleep in their coffins lest their mortality slip their minds and they forget for one moment that *tempus fugit*. We all know that tempus does not fugit except when you're enjoying yourself, just as we know that time can crawl, as it does in a waiting room or an operating room or even a classroom, and that, try as you will to pass that time or, as the saying goes, kill it, it can creep by so slowly that you begin to wonder if your watch has stopped. A night of sweet sleep can pass in the twinkling of an eye while a sleepless one can last an eternity in the same way that a day of hateful labor is immeasurably longer than one filled with activity in which you are intensely interested and totally involved.

Clocks are useful machines for regulating trains and tests and TV programs, for measuring the speed of light or the timing of an egg; they are even nice as *objets d'art* as long as they are seen and not heard, but while they may tell time, they don't tell us anything really meaningful about time, nothing certainly that we can put to any real use in the living of our daily lives. Time is a quantity like water, and whether we measure it out in quarts or coffee spoons, the amounts we divide it up into are amounts of our own devising, for time knows nothing of minutes and hours; it is simply time, and time, after all, does not pass; rather, we pass through time.

The semicolon, ordinarily a misunderstood and overworked punctuation mark, can be used effectively in the Running Style by helping to maintain the momentum that is the hallmark of this style. Since the idea of the Running Style is to avoid as many full stops as possible, the semicolon works in those places where the rule calls for a full stop but where the flow would be interrupted by the use of a period. Notice how this works in the last sentence of the essay. The interrelationship of ideas would be ruined and the effect would be choppy if periods were used. The same can be said for the first sentence of paragraph 3. The point to keep in mind is that nothing must be allowed to let the Running Style run down.

Exercise 4
1. Analyze the diction for liveliness and appropriateness. What about the use of foreign phrases?
2. Explain the subtle transition from a discussion of clocks to a discussion of time in order to understand more fully the inductive process.
3. Write a similar essay in which you ponder one of these curious obsessions: mirrors; moustaches; toy trains; card playing; jogging; collecting autographs; hoarding; photography.

In addition to being a fine style in its own right, the Running Style can also serve as a means of loosening up your writing if you feel it is too cramped or as a way to get started if you suffer from writer's block. It can also serve as a clearing house for ideas that you may wish afterward to reorganize into a more formal style. Of course, as long as it doesn't run away from you, the Running Style can be developed into a very useful medium for the clarification and communication of thoughts and feelings which will only respond to the inductive process. The spontaneity of this style gives it a creative edge that lies beyond learning. You will discover by doing whether or not it is a style that will work for you.

25. The Ironic Style

Irony in writing is the result of an obvious and deliberate contrast between subject matter and treatment. Its effect is humorous and often satirical. Its purpose is to accomplish through a conflict between form and content what you feel you could not do half so well if the two were in harmony, as they are usually supposed to be. If, for example, you felt strongly about gun control but were getting nowhere writing impassioned diatribes supporting it, you could take the opposite view, attack gun control, but do it so flippantly and callously that the reader would know where you stood and be amused, maybe even converted, in the bargain. Or, should you consider some TV show overrated, you could treat it in a lofty manner, praising it as high art, and thus expose its absurdities.

Irony speaks with two tongues, saying one thing on the surface and meaning something else underneath. It's a subtle style because it must betray its meaning without too obviously seeming to do so. Word choice, sound effects, sentence rhythms, and sentence structure all have to be carefully orchestrated so that the reader is sure to read between the lines.

Here is an example of a serious subject treated lightly. The writer is obviously concerned about the irreverent attitude common at funerals and feels the best way to criticize it is to laugh at it.

Funerals are festivities in black. After the shedding of the tears comes the growling of the stomachs. By the time the object of so much grief is safely underground, the grateful survivors are famished. At the sight of a table groaning with food, they fall to with a vengeance. Finally glutted, their spirits animated, they chat excitedly about how good the corpse looked and how sweetly short the service was, each feeling secretly a bit more optimistic about his own immortality.

The word "festivities" tells you right off that this will not be a "grave" approach to the subject, and the alliteration of the "f's" helps. Notice that the alliteration is picked up later on in "famished," "food," and "fall to," subtly connecting the words with "funeral." Another mocking touch is to be found in the parallel phrases in the second sentence (shedding of the tears, growling of the stomachs). The modifiers "safely" and "grateful" in the third sentence continue the mockery. Notice, too, how "grateful," "groaning," and "glutted" are connected. The verb "chat" would hardly be appropriate to respectful conversations about the dead, and "a bit more" has just that touch of light-heartedness the last sentence needs to reinforce its wicked point.

Here is an example of a trivial subject treated seriously. In this case, it is apparent that the writer is amused at the reverential atmosphere attending this rec-room pastime and wishes to poke fun at it by writing about it as if it really mattered.

The fear of stepping on a ping-pong ball haunts the consciousness of even the most seasoned professional and threatens to thwart the noblest efforts to perform well at this demanding sport. Nothing distracts concentration more than the explosion of a ping-pong ball that happens to find its unlucky way under the unwary shoe of the player who is poised for an expert serve or a practiced return. The effect is nerve shattering, and brilliant players have been known to collapse in frenzy over such a disturbance, their confidence destroyed, their hopes for glory dashed.

Although the diction is generally sober, even dramatic, there are two instances where the writer teases the reader with phrases that tell you where his tongue is: "threatens to thwart" which is awful alliteration; and *"unlucky* way under the *unwary* shoe" which heightens the silly image of the runaway ping-pong ball. The parallel inversions of "confidence destroyed" and "glory dashed" end the paragraph on a note of exaggerated misfortune and thus punctuate the ridicule.

Example 1
Here is a trivial subject treated with more importance than it deserves. How soon do you sense the irony? In this selection look especially for the use of aphorisms, always a good device, particularly when you want to sound sententious.

A man is known by the trash he keeps. What to keep and what to discard has been a hoary problem ever since man had to clean his cave. Obviously whatever turns rancid has to go; the dangers to oneself and to others are all too apparent here to be questioned. However, things of sentimental value, like unpaid bills and slivers of soap, are sometimes all too hastily relinquished in moments of reckless house-cleaning. Those who say, "When in doubt, throw it out," forget that memories fade while mementos stay to cheer the fragile heart.

It is better to build another attic than to sacrifice a treasured tennis shoe or a cherished lampshade for the sake of mere space. Attics are the museums of the memory. When all about you crumbles, it is in an attic that you can always find solace. There, among the broken rockers and musty quilts, you can pore over old yearbooks and theatre programs and revive forgotten dreams. Snug in the afterglow of yesteryear, you can rummage among the trinkets and tokens of bygone joys and distant heartaches.

So guard your stuffed drawers and crowded closets, your cluttered basements and littered garages. Remember, he who steals my trash steals, not junk, but the souvenirs of the soul.

Melancholy characterizes the tone of this short essay. It is most apparent in the last sentence of the first paragraph and in all but the first sentence of the second paragraph. Notice such phrases as "memories fade," "cheer the fragile heart," "solace," "forgotten dreams," "snug in the afterglow of yesteryear" (also a play on words), and "bygone joys and distant heartaches."

Exercise 1

1. To what familiar aphorisms do these phrases allude:
   A man is known by the trash he keeps.
   It is better to build another attic . . .
   Attics are the museums of the memory.
   When all about you crumbles . . .
   He who steals my trash . . .
2. Identify outstanding sound effects (alliteration, assonance, consonance, rhythm).
3. Write a short essay in which you treat one of the following trivial topics rather seriously: removing the label from a mattress; changing a lightbulb; opening a child-resistant cap; licking and applying postage stamps; stretching a tea bag. Try to parody aphorisms wherever possible.

Example 2

Here is an important subject treated in an off-hand manner. Like the confessional style, it "gives the writer away," but in this case, the irony is intentional. Look for signals along the way that tell you that the writer is really not kidding herself.

When my husband walked out on me, it hit me like a ton of balloons. I mean, little bubbles began to pop inside my head as one by one the things we had shared burst or blew away. I got out our old wedding pictures and lost myself remembering how tight my gown had been and how worried I was. I had little need to worry, and even less as time went by. My husband was good at telling me that he loved me, but he could never, as Shakespeare said, "suit the action to the word."

At first I admit I was at loose ends, but now I'm getting to like being on my own again. Okay, so I have to fill the bird feeder myself and set the alarm and mix my own martinis, but it has its brighter side, too. No longer do I have to put up with Monday Night Football or ring around the collar. The toughest part, my friends always told me, would be coming home alone to an empty house, but frankly I don't know what they're talking about. Who's alone? I mean, I've got my cat and my TV and my telephone. And I wouldn't call a house *I'm* in exactly empty.

I'll bet it's tougher on him. Nobody to pick up after him. Nobody to do his dirty work. Nobody to blame. My trouble was that I married a stranger who got stranger and stranger. If I miss anything, it's trying to figure him out. Was he deep? Or was he simply an appliance that didn't work—and no guarantee?

Would I take him back? I doubt it. When it comes right down to it, he was harder to live with than without. Meanwhile, though, those old devil balloons keep on a-popping. *Him* desert *me?* What nerve!

Short sentences give this essay its tone of surprised indifference. The staccato pacing suggests brittleness and false courage. What really bothers the writer is that her husband would leave her when she thought she had better cause to leave him. This is the reality she is concealing with her "Who cares?" attitude. She knows the joke's on her, and it's not funny. Notice the shift from "walked out on me" to "desert me."

Exercise 2

1. What is the effect of the series of fragments following the first sentence of paragraph 3?
2. Identify in the opening paragraph at least three clues indicating mixed emotions.
3. Write an essay in which you conceal one of the following worries beneath a frivolous attitude: flunking a course; losing your job; being arrested for shoplifting; drinking too much; betraying a confidence; deceiving someone.

Example 3
Telling an untruth with a straight face is a way of giving the tone of your irony a satiric twist. Here is an example of a "poker-faced lie." What truth lies beneath it? Look closely at the diction.

In the seventies we heard a lot about consciousness raising. Today, more and more people are turning to conscience lowering, or even elimination, as a way of escaping the tedium of guilt. Young moderns are tired of having their fun spoiled by moral hairsplitting. Wondering whether what they are doing is right or wrong robs them, they say, of perfect enjoyment. They're out to stamp out "pangs of conscience," that tiresome phrase so reminiscent of the "hang-ups" of their parents or the "inhibitions" of their grandparents. Today's youth want pure pleasure, unsullied by morbid moralizing. They consider guilt the only sin and are taking pains to eradicate it from their psyches.

Some few lucky persons have grown up with the syndrome and are actively pursuing hitherto proscribed pleasures with no problems whatsoever. A few others find that by running with the "right" crowd, they can quickly overcome the few annoying scruples remaining from a misguided upbringing. Too many, however, despite good intentions, suffer from periodic regression (particularly on Sunday mornings) and are in desperate need of a permanent cure. Fortunately, science has made a major breakthrough in combating this malady, and there is every sign that before the end of the century the last trace of this irritating vestigial remain may disappear from the face of the earth.

The Conscience Lowering Order of Ubiquitous Therapists (CLOUT) has opened an emergency treatment center where intensive care can prevent much of the despair that often affects those stricken with a sudden attack of "the guilts." Massive doses of euphoric drugs and free-wheeling group therapy are turning more and more guilt-free people out onto the streets with less and less recidivism.

The United Nations Conscience Lowering Engineers (UNCLE) have developed a Behavior Modification Program (BMP, or "bump") that promises to silence once and for all that troublesome "wee small voice" that has been identified as the culprit behind this stultifying affliction. Scientists have long suspected its presence, but they have had enormous difficulty isolating it. In spite of the noise it makes, its size is miniscule and its location elusive. Patients who hear it complain that it seems to come from everywhere and nowhere at once. Fortunately, after years of tire-

less, painstaking research, a crack medical team has discovered
that by deadening a section of the brain, the "voice" ceases its
disturbing transmissions.

This operation, however, has not proved to be entirely successful in all cases. Aside from occasional side effects (loss of sight,
hearing, life), it does not seem to work well on elderly people.
"Habits die hard," says one leading pioneer researcher, who ex-
presses the hope that eventually natural mortality will solve the
problem of chronic morality.

Meanwhile, there is new hope for those millions of sufferers
who have been "praying" for a miracle. Once they have undergone this latest therapy, they can join the growing numbers of
happy men and women who are enjoying no-guilt thrills beyond
their wildest fantasies. The only flies in the ointment are the mil-
itant few who stubbornly maintain that guilt increases pleasure.
Many of them belong to archaic religious orders whose "sin and
sob" cycles have conditioned followers to believe that guilt is a
good way to get more mileage out of your sins. Fortunately, the
overwhelming majority of people today save their regret for the
stray sin or two they somehow never quite got around to com-
mitting.

The author of this essay is disturbed by modern immorality, but
instead of attacking it head on, he defends it with such enthusiasm that it collapses under the weight of its own absurdity. The
subject matter here, while not trivial, is certainly ridiculous;
therefore, to handle it ironically, the author takes it all quite
seriously and sees to it that his approach reeks of enlightened
sincerity. Along the way he uses, among other things, two techniques to signal his ironic intentions to the reader. One is the
use of phrases that suggest petulant impatience with any hin-
drance to physical gratification: "the tedium of guilt," "tired of
having their fun spoiled," "moral hairsplitting," "stamp out
'pangs of conscience,' " "unsullied by morbid moralizing," "taking pains to eradicate," "annoying scruples," "misguided upbringing," "irritating vestigial remain," "troublesome 'wee small
voice,' " "stultifying affliction," "no-guilt thrills." The other is

the use of medical and psychological jargon: "consciousness raising," "syndrome," "regression," "permanent cure," "science has
made a major breakthrough in combating this malady," "emergency treatment," "intensive care," "stricken with a sudden attack," "massive doses of euphoric drugs," "free-wheeling group
therapy," "recidivism," "years of tireless, painstaking research,"
"crack medical team," "side effects," "leading pioneer researcher," " 'praying' for a miracle," "latest therapy."

Exercise 3

1. What elements of "bad style" are parodied in the last paragraph? How is the information slanted?
2. What effect do these phrases have on the satiric tone: "tiresome phrase," "annoying scruples," "irritating vestigial remain," "stultifying affliction"?
3. With a straight face, write an essay satirizing one of the following "problems" by seeming to support it: cheating; tax
   evasion; drug pushing; lying; bribery; teenage car theft; ar-
   son.

Example 4

A somewhat tricky variation on being contradictory is the "humorous half-truth." This occurs most often in the form of a joke
someone tells at our expense, assuring us immediately afterwards
that he didn't mean it at all. When that happens, we usually suspect that he meant at least part of what he said. If someone tells
you that you've got a great future behind you, you wonder if he
may have a point. Here is a defense of Scrooge that may strike
you as ridiculous. Can you find a grain of truth in it?

To call Ebenezer Scrooge a miser is to do the poor old man a
gross injustice. Frugal maybe, prudent certainly, but tight-fisted
never. Just because a man who works hard wants to keep what
he earns does not make him a miser. If there is any sin afoot
here, it is Cratchit's envy, not Scrooge's greed. Let those who
covet another man's chattel "sweep before their own doors," as
Goethe said.

Scrooge's reputation has suffered because he lacks what we would call today the right image. He worked too hard, smiled too little, and believed that "the laborer is worthy of his hire." Bob Cratchit might ask for a bit of candle or a lump of coal today, but you can be sure that, if he gets them, he'll be asking for a coffee break tomorrow, a water cooler next week, and a paid vacation next summer. And when he gets that, he'll join a union (or start one) and go out on strike, probably at Christmas time.

We fault Scrooge for his personality, not for any vices. We find him short-tempered, gruff, distant—forgetting that he was a busy man who could not suffer fools gladly. If he wasn't sociable, it's because, as ever, people shun the company of the elderly. His old friends and colleagues were dead, and he was left with only his memories. If some of them were painful and provoked nightmares, does that not call for compassion rather than contempt? If he lived on little food and less heat, is he any different from scores of lonely old people who neglect themselves because others neglect them?

Who goes gently into that good night? Who is safe from fear and regret as the end draws near? To want a second chance is not peculiar to Scrooge, nor is it an admission of guilt. His miserable existence commands our pity, not our scorn. At least Scrooge took care of himself. He was not mealy-mouthing around some welfare office or coughing his life away in some "senior citizens" home, totally dependent on charity. How dare we criticize him for not giving away his security, especially to those who never gave a damn for their own.

How pleased we are when he finally gets spooked enough to play Santa Claus. Today we'd lock him up. Instead, we go him one better and play hypocrite, cheering those on the receiving end (Tiny Tim *et al.*), knowing in our bleeding hearts that Scrooge will wake up the next morning bankrupt, and then where will all the takers be? Let's face it: we're all Scrooges at heart, and when we beat him over the head with the crutch of self-righteousness, it's our own greed we're exorcising. Scrooge is not a sinner; he's a scapegoat.

The author of this essay is only pretending to take Scrooge's part. His point is not to rewrite literary analysis but to make us see that we who scorn Scrooge may do so because he is too much like us. Our self-deception is the real target of this essay, and the author's way of hitting this target is to take a ridiculous point of view and treat it seriously. Notice that this does not mean that there cannot be humor along the way, but notice, too, that the humor is used only when Scrooge's detractors are under attack. It's a literary fugue in which shifts in the content are countered by corresponding shifts in the style. To emphasize that he is writing about us, the author uses such modern imagery and phrasing as "right image," "coffee break," "water cooler," "welfare office," "senior citizens home," "spooked," "bleeding hearts," and "takers."

Exercise 4
1. Explain the connotations of these carefully chosen words:
   frugal . . . prudent . . . tight-fisted
   covet . . . chattel
   short-tempered, gruff, distant
   mealy-mouthing
   the crutch of self-righteousness
   exorcising
2. What is the effect of these quotations and familiar phrases on the style:
   sweep before their own doors
   the laborer is worthy of his hire
   could not suffer fools gladly
   Who goes gently into that good night?
3. Write a satirical defense of one of the following familiar characters in which you are really ridiculing some hypocritical attitude: Simon Legree; Caligula; Richard III; Lady Macbeth; Iago; Charles Manson; Hitler; Jim Jones of Guyana.

Example 5
Sentimentality is not ordinarily intended to be ironic although often it can have an unintentionally ironic effect. Here is an ex-

ample of the deliberate use of sentimentality as a means of accentuating the banality of the subject matter.

There is no sadder sight than that of that forlorn little sophomore girl sitting alone on the sidelines after all her dearest friends have been picked to be cheerleaders. Perhaps she doesn't have the prettiest face, the shapeliest figure, the greatest coordination; what she does have is heart, more heart than all the rest of them, and there she sits, eating it out, while they jump up and down hysterically, torn between starting practice right now or running home to brag. What will Suzy tell her family? How will she hold back the tears and make it all sound as if it doesn't matter when all the time her little heart is breaking and it's the end of the world?

All summer long she practiced and practiced, leaping, straddling, waving, yelling, her muscles aching, her throat parched, her hopes high. There wasn't a yell she didn't know, a routine she hadn't memorized, a cue she hadn't learned. Maybe she wasn't perfect, but what she lacked in skill, she more than made up for in enthusiasm. No team's spirit could have flagged while Suzy was out there bobbing around, screaming her lungs out. Poor, miserable, unselfish Suzy! It wasn't just for herself that she simply had to be a cheerleader. She wanted to win because she wanted her team to win. She knew they needed her, and she was ready to give them her all.

Is there no reward for dedication, for loyalty, for sacrifice? Why must Suzy watch and weep while girls who couldn't care less are chosen on the basis of talents they have done nothing to acquire and do nothing to develop? Suzy is a study in determination. She even paid for and altered her own uniform so that she would be ready the moment they saw how much she had to offer. If there is any justice in this world, if there is recognition for willingness and eagerness and spirit, if the Good Shepherd is minding his flock, then Suzy will surely survive this dark hour and live to see a brighter day.

Clichés give this essay the false note it needs to cheapen the sentiment: "no sadder sight," "her dearest friends," she has "heart"

and she is "eating it out" even while it is "breaking," "hopes
high," "ready to give them her all," "reward for dedication,"
"couldn't care less," "a study in determination," "if there is any
justice in this world," "this dark hour," and "live to see a brighter
day."

Exercise 5
1. What phrases tell us the truth about the reasons for Suzy's
   failure?
2. What phrases suggest an uncharitable attitude on Suzy's part?
3. Write an essay in which you wax sentimental about one of the
   following trivial disappointments: not getting what you wanted
   for Christmas; not being rushed by a particular fraternity or
   sorority; having your favorite TV program preempted; not
   being "carded" at a bar; your first gray hair.

Example 6
An experiment similar to the one described below was actually
conducted not too long ago. The whole thing was so foolish that
there was no way to write a serious report about it and not sound
ironic. As you analyze the following rendition, notice how the
use of colorless jargon to circumscribe the silliness only widens
the gap between form and content and enhances the ironic effect.
Since, unfortunately, it is not uncommon for silly subjects to be
written about seriously in an attempt to hoodwink the reader (an
abuse of style), this report has the added charm of parodying the
very style it is written in.

Laboratory experiments intended to test physical response to
centerfold stimuli have been accelerated as a result of the increase
in both the number and cooperation of the volunteers. There are
currently ten male volunteers who operate in relays within the
testing area. As his turn comes, each volunteer is strapped into a
specially constructed chair designed in such a way as to permit
him to do nothing but concentrate on the pictures that are flashed
on the screen erected in front of him. Electrodes are attached to

all pertinent neurological areas of the body so that each response may be recorded on highly sensitive instruments.

A certain reluctance to terminate the prescribed testing period has been noted among several particularly virile volunteers, even when the instruments indicate that the volunteer has entered the zone of desensitivity and reduced response capability. The tension created between the reluctance of one volunteer to desist and the eagerness of the next volunteer to proceed has had its effect on the neurological data, but steps are being taken to separate aggressive behavior exhibited towards a sexual stimulus from aggressive behavior exhibited towards a sexual rival. At this point there is some reason to believe that the two are not necessarily discrete attitudinal responses. Continued tests should either confirm or refute this hypothesis.

The use of the passive voice (have been accelerated . . . is strapped . . . are flashed . . . are attached . . . may be recorded . . . has been noted . . . are being taken) lends a note of false detachment to the pseudo-scientific coolness of the tone. It is important that the tone be consistently sober. One smirk and the effect would be ruined, just as a joke is ruined when the teller laughs while telling it.

Exercise 6

1. Translate the following euphemisms:
   pertinent neurological areas
   reluctance to terminate
   zone of desensitivity and reduced response capability
   discrete attitudinal responses
2. Are there any double-meanings? If so, do they harm the effect?
3. Write a similar report of one of the following imaginary experiments. As you pit style against content, parody that style by using the jargon and euphemisms of relevant disciplines (business, psychology, sociology, etc.).

   a. the effect of three-button coats on sales resistance
   b. the effect of an all-jello diet on aggressive behavior

c. the effect of lighting the wrong end of a filter cigarette on self-image
d. the effect of doorbell chimes on social behavior
e. the effect of long underwear on creativity

Writing ironically is the severest test of style because it requires you to keep form, content, and audience at harmonious odds with each other. In the last essay, for example, what is said is silly, the way it is said is stuffy, and the ordinary reader of such a report is not the one intended to read this one. However, the friction produced when form opposes content attracts the kind of reader who would scorn both separately but who is amused when they are combined. The Ironic Style is a juggling act, and even if you are not always successful at it, there is no better way to remain alert to the delicate balance between style, subject matter, and reader than to practice it. This balance is the essence of good style. If you know how to say what you want to say to the people you want to say it to, then they're going to say that you do have a way with words.

Index